W9-AOM-912

Travels in Mexico and California

NUMBER TEN
*Essays on the American West, sponsored by
the Elma Dill Russell Spencer Foundation*

Asa Bement Clarke

Travels in Mexico and California

COMPRISING A JOURNAL OF A TOUR FROM BRAZOS SANTIAGO,
THROUGH CENTRAL MEXICO, BY WAY OF MONTEREY,
CHIHUAHUA, THE COUNTRY OF THE APACHES, AND THE
RIVER GILA, TO THE MINING DISTRICTS OF CALIFORNIA

By A. B. Clarke

EDITED BY ANNE M. PERRY

TEXAS A&M UNIVERSITY PRESS
COLLEGE STATION

Originally published by the author in 1852
and produced by Wright & Hasty, Printers, Boston

The paper used in this book meets the minimum requirements
of the American National Standard for Permanence
of Paper for Printed Library Materials, Z39.48-1984.
Binding materials have been chosen for durability.

Library of Congress Cataloging-in-Publication Data

Clarke, A. B. (Asa Bement), 1817–1882.
   Travels in Mexico and California: comprising a journal of a tour from Brazos Santiago
through central Mexico by way of Monterey, Chihuahua, the country of the Apaches, and
the River Gila to the mining districts of California/by A. B. Clarke: edited by Anne M.
Perry.—1st ed.
      p.   cm.—(Essays on the American West; no. 10.)
   "Originally published in 1852 by Wright & Hasty, printers, Boston"—T.p. verso.
   Bibliography: p.
   Includes index.
   ISBN 0-89096-354-1 (alk. paper):
      1. Clarke, A. B. (Asa Bement), 1817– 1882—Diaries.   2. Clarke, A. B. (Asa
Bement), 1817– 1882—Journeys—California.   3. Southwest, New—Description and
travel.   4. Mexico—Description and travel.   5. California—Gold discoveries—
History—19th century.   6. California—Description and travel—1848–1869.
I. Perry, Anne, 1943–   .   II. Title.   III. Series.
F786.C57 1988
917.2′ 046—dc19   88-1490
                                                                                      CIP

Contents

Illustrations

Preface

AN ESTIMATED three hundred thousand men, women, and children traveled the overland route to California in the decade following the discovery of gold at Sutter's Mill in 1848.[1] Others went West along different routes across the continent, across Central America, and around Cape Horn. Some fifteen thousand emigrants a year traveled the routes through Mexico during 1849 and 1850. After that, "the hardships of the route(s) had been sufficiently publicized so that relatively few followed in later years."[2] Estimates of trail mortality vary widely, ranging from below John Unruh's figure of ten thousand (4 percent of participants) to thirty thousand.[3]

What accounts for the mass migration from established jobs and families to the West? The lure of gold encouraged the press to print a great deal of information about the goldfields and how to get to them. By late 1848, the existence of abundant gold in California had been verified by authorities, and many newspapers had regular articles of interest to prospective gold seekers.

Edwin Bryant's *What I Saw in California*, in addition to newspaper reports, provided much of the information available about California. Bryant, who had traveled to California in 1846–47 and was on a speaking tour of the East when news of the gold strike arrived, quickly found himself in great demand. The following excerpt from one of his speeches gives a flavor of the Gold Rush hysteria:

> The buzz of the New York Stock Exchange is in California. The hotels, railway-cars, steam-boats and omnibuses ring with its wonders; and in every place where congregations, great or small get together, the one and pervading topic refers to the new region of hope and expectation. Everybody seems to be going or sending

there; groups of people assemble at street-corners, organizing emigration parties; every grog shop has its Californian club; ship-brokers are worried to death by applicants entreating to be sailed, gold hunting, and woe betide the man who is known to have had any direct or indirect communication with San Francisco. . . . Fleets of ships are announced as about to make flying passages to the regions of bliss; the newspapers teem with advertisements referring to the requirements of emigrants.[4]

By early 1849, several journals and guides described travel to California. The majority described northern overland routes. Perhaps the availability of advice about these routes explains their popularity.

Additionally, evidence published later in many journals and books about the Gold Rush suggests that a number of the men were caught up by the accounts and advertisements of relatively easy travel to the goldfields. They did not pay adequate attention to warnings of hardships. Many, if not most, thought they were participating in Manifest Destiny and embarking on an adventure with little danger and would return with massive fortunes. Some men carefully organized and planned their trips based on any information they could acquire. Others pushed toward California without reflection and suffered the consequences. Even with excellent planning, emigrants faced many hardships.

Those who were interested in the southern routes had Emory's report of Kearny's 1846 reconnaissance and newspaper accounts of Cooke's and Graham's routes. In addition, many of the men in mining companies that traveled along the southern trails through Mexico had recently returned from fighting in the Mexican War and were held in high regard by their traveling companions. These veterans were thought to be knowledgeable about the trek. Their stories of battles appear in many journals as witness to the respect in which the forty-niners held them. These men chose southern routes to avoid the horrors of early snows and blocked mountain passes, as well as other disasters.

Three major trailblazers preceded the Argonauts of 1849 who traveled the southern routes. One of them was Brig. Gen. Stephen Watts Kearny. Journal writers Lt. Col. W. H. Emory and Henry Smith Turner traveled with Kearny in 1846. They were followed within weeks by Lt. Col. Philip St. George Cooke and the Mormon Battalion, which had traveled from Nauvoo, Illinois. Maj. Lawrence P. Graham, with journal writer Cave Johnson Couts and the Second Dragoons, traveled from Monterrey, Mexico, to California at the end of the Mexican War in 1848. At least some of the men had access to Emory's and Cooke's comments about their routes, since some journals mention those sources. Emory's "Notes of a Military Reconnoissance, from Fort Leavenworth, in Missouri, to San Diego, in California, including Part of the Arkansas, Del Norte, and Gila Rivers," was published in 1848.

Journals written by others accompanying Kearny, Cooke, and Graham were not available to Gold Rush participants, but newspaper accounts and many maps were published to meet public demand. Unfortunately, some of the maps were inaccurate and led to more than a few deaths. The time of year affected the availability of water and food for both men and animals on all cross-continent routes. During some seasons, marked wells were found dried up or polluted, and watersheds would be raging rivers or bone dry. Grass was practically nonexistent over long stretches of the southern routes in some seasons.

When Benjamin Hayes was crossing the Colorado River below its junction with the Gila River at the end of 1849, he was told by Colonel Corrasco of the Mexican army that about twelve thousand emigrants had crossed at that point during the year. Only about half of those were Americans; the rest were Sonorans.[5] Of those six thousand Americans, relatively few kept journals, making journals of the southern trails very valuable. Some of the 1849 emigrants whose travel accounts of the southern routes were later published include Lorenzo D. Aldrich, John Woodhouse Audubon, Robert Brownlee, Robert Eccleston, George B. Evans, and Benjamin

Butler Harris. Evidence suggests that A. B. Clarke was one of the earliest of the Gold Rush emigrants who kept and published a journal of the southern trail adventures.[6]

Men from almost every state and Europe came to California during the Gold Rush. Haskins, in *The Argonauts of California*, lists the men in the "mining company from Springfield," including Clarke, and under Capt. J. F. Harding, as leaving from New York on January 28. Haskins also lists some of these men and others as leaving on the schooner *John Castner,* which sailed January 29.[7]

Just two days later, Dr. J. E. Field and other members of the North Adams, Massachusetts, Company left New York on the schooner *C. G. Scull.*[8] Dr. Field had survived the Goliad massacre as a surgeon in Fannin's command during the Texas fight for independence from Mexico in 1836. He had returned to Massachusetts and published a book about his adventures in Texas, had spent time practicing medicine in Texas, and was now ready, apparently, for another adventure. Though he traveled from a location very near Clarke's home in Massachusetts at approximately the same time and along the same route as Clarke, evidence does not indicate that the two men ever met until near the Pima Indian villages on the Gila River. From there, they traveled as messmates, and Dr. Field probably had some influence in the first publication of Clarke's book.

Clarke also mentions John E. Durivage in his journal. The two traveled in close proximity, with Governor McNees' wagons, from Janos to Warner's Rancho.[9] Durivage, a correspondent for the *Daily Picayune* in New Orleans, Louisiana, had been in Texas and Mexico during the Mexican War, was infected with gold fever, and left New Orleans for California on March 4, 1849. He reached Brazos Santiago on March 10. His letters and journal are contained in Ralph P. Bieber's *Southern Trails to California in 1849.*

The United States had just won the Mexican War in 1848, and many Mexican nationals were resentful. The relationship between Mexicans and Americans was further strained because most emigrants adopted a suspicious attitude toward the Mexicans and expected the worst from them. However, from Monterrey Durivage wrote:

> There are quite a number of Americans here, toward whom the Mexicans are all very well disposed; in fact, throughout the entire length of this line the Americans are respected if they are respectable. It affords me pleasure to say that there have been no complaints made against emigrants passing along this route to California. They have behaved themselves and respected the Mexicans, and have consequently left a most favorable impression wherever they have passed. [10]

There were stories in many Gold Rush journals about thievery by the Mexicans and the necessity of mounting guards to prevent the loss of property. Clarke's descriptions of Mexican people were typical of those found in journals about the southern routes during that period. Fortunately, he was treated most hospitably when he stayed in the *alcalde*'s home in Janos and seemed genuinely impressed by the kindness and generosity of the *alcalde*'s family.

Similarly, word about Indians had spread to Americans from military reconnaissances, Mexicans, and earlier emigrants. The sentiment that Indians could not be trusted and that one need not be frank with them was commonly held by American military personnel and emigrants. Lieutenant Cooke's strategy of appearing to make common cause with each side in the continuing war between Mexicans and Apaches seemed to be excellent from a military point of view. The other tribes along the southern trails were treated according to rumors spread about them. There was also evidence that later emigrants were treated very badly by Indians, perhaps because of growing numbers of atrocities committed against the Indians by American and Mexican scalp hunters.

The purpose of this republication is to make Clarke's record of traveling the southern route to California as a member of the 1849 Gold Rush more available for historical study. His notes, taken faithfully each day, bring meaning to forty-niners' fear of dying from cholera, Indian attack, starvation, or thirst on *jornada*s through the deserts.[11] Clarke presents detailed observations of the country's physical environment and of the life-styles, economic status, and ways of life of the local inhabitants, both Indian and Mexican.

The original text is reproduced here in its entirety. Editorial comment has been designed to clarify the text. Words have been explained only if their meaning is not clear in context.

Journals and maps from the 1849 Gold Rush period contain many variations in spelling. Perhaps because Clarke was a teacher, few such errors appear in his journal, except for the names of places and people. Spellings that seem phonetically clear, such as "Ca-manches" (Comanches) and "chapparal" (chaparral) have received no editorial comment. In each case, the version of names used by Clarke has been retained.

Similarly, Clarke's system of punctuation reflects the correct usage of his times and has been retained. Spanish words that are not commonly recognized appear in italics and, where possible, are defined. On rare occasion, obvious printer's errors are corrected. Otherwise, corrections and clarifications in Clarke's text appear in brackets, through use of [*sic*], or in notes. Additionally, notes contain information on the people, places, and subjects that Clarke mentions. Minimal editorial correction has been made to quotations in notes.

I wish to express my gratitude to my stepfather, Robert S. Hovey, who first gave me his great-grandfather A. B. Clarke's journal to read for a report when I was in ninth grade, almost thirty years ago. It fascinated me then and has helped me understand why students need access to original sources for historical study. When the possibility of republishing the journal came up, he was thorough in his own investigations and assistance. Other Clarke family members who have been very helpful include Mrs. Joseph M. (Constance Clarke) Myers, Mrs. Charles F. (Josephine Clarke) Grey, and John G. Shellito, M.D. Mrs. Myers found the will that Clarke wrote in Brownsville when he was afraid of dying of chol-

era and the photographs we have used. Dr. Shellito provided
the copies of Clarke's original passport and certificate of U.S.
citizenship.

In editing and annotating this volume, I consulted a wide
variety of source material. I would like to express my appreciation
to archivists at the Barker Texas History Center of the University of
Texas at Austin; Peter Blodgett, assistant curator of western manu-
scripts at the Henry E. Huntington Library in San Marino, California; James D. Hofer and Daniela Moneta, archivists and librarians at the Southwest Museum in Los Angeles, California;
Judy Sheldon at the California Historical Society's Schubert Hall
Library in San Francisco; and librarians at the Bancroft Library of
the University of California at Berkeley. I am also grateful to Dr.
William H. Goetzmann, who spent precious time listening and
giving advice during my unannounced visit to his office early in my
research. Memories of his office at the University of Texas at Austin
continue to be an inspiration to me.

Finally, I would like to thank my husband Frank, and our
children, Kris and Tad, for their continuing support and patience
as my professional work continues.

Biographical Introduction

ASA BEMENT CLARKE, the author of this journal, was a farmer, student, teacher, and drugstore owner before starting West. Many experiences in his life instilled in him independence and a love of travel. He was born the third boy in a family of four boys and three girls on June 8, 1817, in Conway, Massachusetts.

His father, Ebenezer Clarke, was a farmer. He died from injuries suffered when he fell out of a tree while he and Asa, then age fifteen, were gathering apples. Asa later wrote:

> When on his death bed, my father made his will. I was asked whether I would stay on the farm with brother Rodolphus or get an education. Being naturally fond of learning, I replied without much thought that I would get an education. Whether I was wise in my choice I have never been able fully to determine, though it is certain that I have a taste for agriculture and its pursuits. . . .
>
> By the conditions [of the will], I was to assist my brother on the farm till eighteen years of age. After that time I was at liberty to commence a Classical education. [1]

During the first ten years after he left the farm, he alternately taught school (usually during the winter term) and attended school or traveled. Schools he attended included Mr. Clary's Good English Classical School in Conway, Castleton Seminary, and Amherst College (for two months in October of 1837).[2] Later he wrote, "In order to get along as to pecuniary affairs, it would have been necessary to teach school nearly every winter. Everything considered I have never been sorry that I left college; let others think as they may, I think I have decided taste for the languages, especially the Latin, which I have read constantly since I left college."[3]

His mother, Sally Griffith Clarke, died in 1837, when he was

twenty. Her death probably compelled him to concentrate more on
supporting himself and less on continuing his studies. His two
months at Amherst College later that year were his last formal
studies. His older sister Almira and her husband, O. N. Stoddard,
wrote him in February of 1838. She chastised him for not writing
to her in over a year and for leaving college:

> Now if you really think it best to leave college and wish to
> teach, let us know your wishes and if you would prefer a warmer
> climate, I think Virginia would suit you. I will most gladly do
> any thing in my power for you. But why, dear A., do you give up
> study? I thought you a studious boy and had set my heart upon
> your receiving a first rate education and [am] utterly at a loss to
> conceive the reason of the change in your plans. Do open to me
> frankly all your mind; tell me as freely as you used to do what are
> your hopes and what are your wishes. You know not how much I
> feel interested in your future welfare.

Almira's husband added:

> I am sorry to hear you have left college. Is your determination
> fixed? Or is it a temporary withdrawal only? Do not become dis-
> couraged at any obstruction whatever. There are none which
> cannot be surmounted. Their existence is often a blessing, trials
> have given to the world some of the brightest minds that have
> shone in science, literature, and theology. No distinguished ge-
> nius can be made without them. As well might the metals be
> purified without fire—besides it is the hottest fire that produces
> the purest and brightest of earth's treasures. Perhaps few have
> struggled with greater difficulties in acquiring an education than
> myself. I have seen times when every way seemed shut up and
> every avenue closed, but light has always succeeded darkness. Put
> on courage and go ahead if you wish come South, we will assist
> you as much as possible. (Letter written by Almira and O. N.
> Stoddard, February 21, 1838, Isle of Wight County, Smithfield,
> Virginia, to Asa B. Clarke, Conway, Franklin County, Massachu-
> setts, in care of R. Clarke.)

A. B. Clarke had taken a school at Rochester Center for the winter term, and during that time made up his mind to go to Virginia to teach school. He returned home for his clothing and a visit with his brother Rodolphus and friends, then he left for Virginia. The letter from his sister and brother-in-law may have influenced his decision to go.

Clarke's love for history is mentioned in his autobiographical account. During his travels, he always took time to visit historical sites. On the way to Virginia, he passed through Baltimore and commented, "During my stay, as is my custom, I traveled the city pretty thoroughly." [4]

When Clarke was eleven, he suffered a concussion and nearly died when he fell from a horse-drawn wagon, and during travels after his parents' deaths, he had several alarming experiences on boat trips. These and other events may have left him feeling confident that he could survive almost any hardship. [5]

He moved with seeming ease from one teaching situation to another. Clarke reported that he received $13.50 per month and board during the first quarter he taught in Conway. In West Springfield, he received $15 and board, and in Rochester, he received $25 and board. In Fincastle, Virginia, he received $500 per year as salary. When not teaching, he traveled extensively in each region.

In a letter to his brother Rodolphus in Conway, Massachusetts, posted from Campbell Court House, Virginia, June 15, 1843, Clarke wrote:

> I shall not take much vacation this summer, but intend to attend closely to teaching this year, and hope by the expiration of another to finish my school teaching.
>
> They want me to go back to my last year's situation and stay another year, but if I go on as I have done from year to year I shall find myself an old bachelor, superanuated and broken down, before I know it. Still I am sometimes loth to quit. The greatest vexation and the greatest tax upon my patience is striving to learn the careless and dull.

In January, 1845, he left his last school for Westfield, Massachusetts, where in March, he purchased a drugstore and took possession immediately. "This is the kind of business which suited me very well," he wrote.[6] With the increased competition of a third apothecary shop in town, he demonstrated good business skills, since he "continued to get in a better assortment of goods as trade increased." In 1847 or 1848, he also established a drugstore at Palmer Depot.

One genealogist (who wrote the information in the *Conway, Massachusetts, Vital Records to 1850*) reports that he married twice before heading West. Family records dispute this, since no mention of any wives except Margaret Hedges exists. Whether or not he knew Margaret Hedges before his travels to California is unclear from his writing. However, Joseph Hedges, Jr., one of Margaret's cousins, left for California with a group from Springfield (near Westfield), including Clarke, on January 28, 1849. In the 1852 census in San Francisco County, a Joseph Hedges, age twenty-seven, occupation wheelwright, who was born in Massachusetts and listed his residence as Massachusetts, was recorded.

A letter written to Margaret Hedges Clarke by Joseph Hedges, dated January 11, 1852, from Stockton, stated:

> It appears that you have met with the same success [marriage] that our cousin L. has. Little did I think when we were travilling in Mexico that one of our company would so soon become Cousin Asa. Freaquently we use to talk who would be married and who would not. I remember well of making a bet with Parker in Mexico in regard to Juliett and Asa getting married. It seems he (Parker) has won the bet.

In 1848, Clarke was a proven entrepreneur in the drugstore trade in Westfield, Massachusetts. He was single and interested in traveling and history. He probably read the increasing number of accounts of the California gold mines with great interest. In August, 1849, nearing the end of his trip to California, he wrote, "As one object in taking this trip was for the travel it afforded, now it is over, I do not regret it, as I think that I have been amply repaid."[7]

Whether Clarke's main interest in going to California was to establish a trading position or actually to mine is unknown, but he traveled about to do some mining. At the same time, he was probably trying to find the most likely sites for trading, and he eventually established a general store in Marysville, an "advantageous site at the confluence of the Yuba with the Feather River. It was a natural point at which to found a city for the distribution of supplies to the mines in the great districts to the north and the east."[8]

In 1936, Clarke's daughter, Fanny E. Clarke, wrote the following in a pamphlet, "A Short Sketch of Our Branch of the Clarke Family":

My father did very little actual mining for gold, but opened up a store at Marysville, near Sacramento. He sold miners supplies, etc., which sold for fabulous prices. One thing I remember his telling us about. He received a shipment of miners scales (around the Horn I suppose) through his brother Lincoln. They cost him $1.00 apiece and they sold for $15.00 apiece. In some of the mining camps vegetables were at a premium. An onion would sell for $1.00 and other things in proportion. After remaining in California a year or more he returned to Westfield to look after his interests there. He was somewhat of a hero in the eyes of his young lady acquaintances, my mother among the number, as he had been so far away in unknown lands.[9]

Clarke left the store in Marysville in the care of his brother-in-law William Bartlett (his sister Aurora's widower) in March, 1851, and returned to Westfield. The 1850 Census of California, Sacramento County, on November 22, listed in one household: Lorenzo D. Ladd, age twenty-eight, no trade, from Vermont; Wm. Bartlett, age thirty-five, trader, from Massachusetts; and Asa D. [sic] Clarke, age thirty-three, trader, from Massachusetts. "The entire stock [of the store] was afterwards burned and he never returned to California."[10]

A letter written by Bartlett in Marysville, to Clarke on De-

cember 1, 1851, gave the following account of business and the
fire:

> Our business was a large and as profitable as any house in town
> up to the 30th of Aug., the night of the fire, an (account) of which
> no doubt you have seen. The amt of our loss including Stock and
> Building and fixtures was about $26000. We lost $7000 worth of
> liquors, nearly $2000 of Butter. We saved about $3000, $1500
> of which was sold the day before to one of our customers and paid
> for and the proceeds invested that day in flour.
>
> We went to bed worth $18000 and at 2 o'clock waked up
> finding ourselves after paying our debts $2000 worse than noth-
> ing. Such are the vicissitudes of trade in this country. If we had
> made this amt of money by speculation I should not have looked
> upon it as quite so hard a case, but every dollar of it had been
> earned in a fair, honorable course of trade.
>
>   . . . You would perhaps like some of the particulars of the fire.
> It commenced on High Street with the wind from the N.W. it
> burnt the Block fronting the plaza on the north also the block
> fronting on the east also on 1st st on both sides of the st for the
> distance of two squares back. The whole amount of property
> burnt was not less than $500,000. The losses among your ac-
> quaintances were C. Lambit $15000. Low & Brothers $10000.
> Farish & Adams $25000. F. W. Shafer $2000. Iewitt & Chuseman
> & Kasson & Beach about $10000 each. K. B. Kent, Bartlett &
> Co $26000. All the gambling houses were burnt.

In the available family records, there is no mention of how
Clarke returned to the East in March, 1851. In a letter sent to
Clarke at Sutter's Fort, dated April 24, 1849, his brother Albert in
Conway, Massachusetts, wrote the following advice:

> Come home when the rainy season sets in, even if you should not
> get gold enough to defray expenses. A winter in California is both
> uncomfortable and unprofitable. You can undoubtedly then re-
> turn without hindrance by the Isthmus route. I should suppose,
> from what I learn, that the chances to return directly were, even
> now, good. There being more vessels, of course, on the Gulf of
> Mexico than in the Pacific.

It is therefore likely that he crossed the Isthmus of Panama.
Margaret Hedges and Asa B. Clarke were married at Westfield
on October 15, 1851. They lived a while with her parents, and
their first child, Virginia, was born on September 6, 1852.
Family records show that Clarke was influenced by his cousin,
Judge Clarke of Dubuque, Iowa, and his brother Albert to move
West. Albert wrote a letter in July, 1852 recommending the
move. He also wrote about Clarke's journal publication:

> I am glad you think of publishing your Journal. Merriam of
> Springfield or Jewett & Co of Cornhill, Boston will (either) be
> good places to get it done. I think I advised you to have it bound
> in the form of Harpers Magazine & get copies enough printed to
> make the business pay by selling them at the common cheap rate.
> You must not expect to make much money, but, were it my own
> case, I should do it, if I could make it pay & make nothing. I
> should not think there would be any risk in this course. You must
> look well to the proof sheets, for prints make blunders if not
> corrected. Your title page strikes me well enough. Perhaps your
> introduction might be corrected thus. . . . As this journal was
> primarily written for the use of a few friends, it may not in all
> respects be suited to the public taste: but as it is descriptive of a
> portion of country but little known to Americans, the author has
> been induced to make it public, & hopes it will not be found
> wanting in interest to the indulgent reader.

In the spring of 1853, the family took the railroad to the end of
the line, in Rockford, Illinois, and from there they traveled by
stage to Dubuque. "The roads were terrible and the stages ran
irregularly. Sometimes they would get to a place and expect to
spend the night there when along would come the next stages and
they would have to pack up again bag and baggage, baby and all
and go on." [11]
Clarke studied law with Judge Dyer in Dubuque and was
admitted to the bar. He also joined his brother Albert in the real
estate business there.
By the fall of 1854, Clarke, his wife and daughter, and Albert

Margaret Hedges Clarke

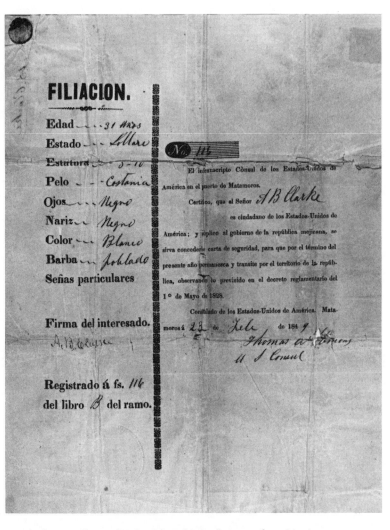

FILIACION.

Edad _ _ _ _ _ . *31 Años*

Estado _ _ _ _ *Soltero*

Estatura _ _ _ _ *5-10*

Pelo _ _ _ _ *Castaño*

Ojos _ _ _ _ *Negro*

Nariz _ _ _ _ *Negro*

Color _ _ _ _ *Blanco*

Barba _ _ _ _ *Poblado*

Señas particulares

Firma del interesado.

A. B. Clarke

Registrado á fs. *116*
del libro *B* del ramo.

N° *116*

El infrascripto Cònsul de los Estados-Unidos de América en el puerto de Matamoros.

Certifico, que el Señor *A B Clarke* es ciudadano de los Estados-Unidos de América; y suplico al gobierno de la república mejicana, se sirva concederle carta de seguridad, para que por el término del presente año permanezca y transite por el territorio de la república, observando lo prevenido en el decreto reglamentario del 1° de Mayo de 1828.

Consulado de los Estados-Unidos de América. Matamoros á *22* de *Juli* de 184*9*

Thomas & Simons
U S Consul

Clarke's certificate of U.S. citizenship and request for a Mexican passport

ESTADO LIBRE DE TAMAULIPAS.

El Ciudadano *Carlos Franc.ᵒ Galbert* ————
Alcalde 3.ᵖ Constitucional de esta Ciudad y Puerto de Matamoros

N. 236.

Concedo libre y seguro pasaporte al
*Sor Dⁿ A. B. Clarke Ciudadano
de los EEUU.*
para que pueda pasar á *California cu-
yo individuo tiene solicitado un Orite
de seguridad segun el adjunto Certificado*

FILIACION.

Edad, *31 años*
Estatura, *5. 10*
Color, *Blanco*
Ojos, *Negros*
Nariz, *Regular*
Pelo, *Castaño*
Barba, *Poblada*
Señas particulares,

llevando para la defensa de su persona las
armas necesarias.
Por tanto: mando á los encargados de
justicia de mi jurisdiccion, ruego y encargo
á las autoridades civiles y militares, no le
pongan embarazo en su transito, y sí le fran-
queen los auxilios que pida, pagándolos por
sus justos precios.
Dado en el Puerto de Matamoros á *23*
de *Feb.ᵒ* ——— de 184*2*

Firma del interesado
A. B. Clarke

Carlos F. Galbert

Clarke's Mexican passport

Clarke's will, made before leaving Brownsville, Texas, February 24, 1849. The text of it reads: "In case that I should not live to return to Westfield or shall not otherwise direct. I give to my brother E. L. Clarke all my books, clothing, furniture, watch, arms & equipment & one hundred dollars. The balance of my property to be divided equally among my three brothers, E. Lincoln, Albert & Rodolphus. I make this request thinking that it will be satisfactory to all as I sign in the presence of Mr. Gilbert. I think that brother Lincoln needs assistance more than my other two brothers. A. B. Clarke."

VIEW OF THE CONFLAGRATION OF MARYSVILLE, ON THE NIGHT OF AUGUST 30th 1851.

Three entire squares consumed. — Loss estimated $ 500,000.   Bancroft Library

Published by R.A.Eddy, Stationers Warehouse, Marysville, Cal.ª

Lith. by Justh, Quirot & Cº California St. corn. Montg.y St. S.Francisco

The great Marysville, California, fire in 1851. (Courtesy the Bancroft Library)

were in Independence, Iowa. They helped organize the Pres-
byterian church there in 1855. In Independence Clarke success-
fully engaged in real estate, farming, and the drug and grocery
business.

He traveled very little after moving to Independence. The only
two trips noted in family papers are with Margaret to the Centennial in Philadelphia in 1876 and to New Orleans on a pleasure
trip in 1881. He died after a three-day illness, described by
Fanny as "something like a congestive chill" with periods of
unconsciousness, on December 27, 1882, and was buried in
Independence.

Travels in Mexico and California

Note

As this Journal was primarily written for the use of a few friends, doubtless many of the incidents may be too particularzied for public taste, but as the route is through a portion of country but little known to Americans, the Author has been induced to publish it, and hopes it will not be found wanting in interest to the general reader.

A. B. C.

Westfield, July 2nd, 1852.

January 29—February 21, 1849

JAN. 29TH, 1849. The Hampden Mining Company, numbering forty-six, took passage on board the schooner Jno.
Castner, at New York, bound for Brazos Santiago. There were also on board
several small companies, from N.Y. and Conn., in all numbering
about one hundred. We were conducted to Sandy Hook by a Steam
towboat.

A large concourse of people had assembled to witness our depar-
ture. At 12 o'clock, M., being ready, we left the wharf amidst the
cheering of friends, which was answered heartily by those on
board, and as long as friends could recognize each other, between
the vessel and shore, there was waving of handkerchiefs and other
tokens of recognition. One of the company, in the mean time, had
stationed himself on the quarterdeck, with the flag of our country
streaming in the wind, and others had formed a little musical band
and were playing some lively airs.

On reaching Sandy Hook, the boat left us to make our way
alone, and having a fine breeze, we were soon out of sight of land.
Our party was principally from Westfield, and Springfield, Mass.,
and vicinity. We had sent a Mr. Brooks, from N.Y. by way of
New Orleans, to purchase mules for the company, in Texas. He
was to have them driven to Point Isabel, at which place we were to
meet him.

JAN. 30TH. Out of sight of land. The greater part of the passengers sea-sick.

JAN. 31ST. Rainy, rough and boisterous. We are kept on what is
called seamen's fare. No bread but hard navy bread. The water
positively horrible. Salt beef and pork every day, and for a change, a
kind of thick soup which they call lob skous.

FEB. 1ST. The weather is still boisterous and the sea rough, and it makes a desperate time for the uninitiated landsmen on this worst of seas, in the worst of seasons, in want of every comfort. Some of us, however, occasionally remember our friends by repairing to a box of delicacies, which they have provided. FEB. 2D. 12 M. lat. 32° 8′. The sun rose this morning in all his splendor. He was hailed by us all with great delight, as it was the first time that we had the pleasure of seeing him since leaving N.Y. FEB. 3D. After a very windy night, the sun rose as brightly as on the previous morning. I have eaten nothing worth mentioning, for the last four days. The passengers complain bitterly of the hard fare. Just before sundown we passed and spoke the sch. Denmark, of Boston. Evening beautiful. FEB. 4TH. Becalmed, opposite the coast of Florida. The sea is as tranquil as a glassy lake, and the air so mild and genial that the passengers lie stretched over the deck in their loose coats. Most of them are reading, and it is pleasing to observe, that many of them are reading the bible. Considering the various characters collected together, the passengers are spending the day, (Sabbath,) as appropriately as could be expected. I notice that those who are addicted to the use of profane language, refrain, in a great measure, on this day. Some are perusing neatly bound books, perhaps the gifts of dear friends at parting. There are a number of young men, formerly of the army in Mexico, who are able to give us some information concerning the country and its inhabitants.

The evening was one of the most beautiful that I ever experienced, and giving myself up to reflections on the past, my thoughts involuntarily turned to home, the scenes of my childhood, and the events of a life that have been somewhat varied. FEB. 5TH. To-day, we entered the trade winds. Flying-fish are seen in great numbers. Passed a bucket floating on the water. No vessel in sight. A strong breeze sprang up in the night, which sent us rapidly on our course. A flying-fish was picked up on deck this morning. At 11 o'clock, Abaco, one of the Bermudas, was discovered, which was the first land seen since leaving Sandy Hook. Towards night we passed the Hole in the Wall, and Abaco Light-

House. This Hole in the Wall, is a remarkably arched passage, through a ledge of rocks which are detached from the shore. It is so large that small vessels can pass through, and is a noted landmark for sailors. All hands on deck, and in the rigging, enjoying the sight of land, from which breezes, balmy with the perfume of vegetation, were floating. The musicians were playing some lively music. All wished that a little time could be given to enjoy the fruits and delightful climate of these islands, at this season. At dark spoke the brig Santiago, from Cadiz. The captain inquired who was the president of the U.S.

FEB. 7TH. At 1 o'clock last night we passed the Berry Islands. This morning, the pig which had made himself familiar with all on board, was killed, and we had him served up for dinner. All engaged in preparing saddles and trappings for mules, tents, &c. Passing over the Bahama Banks. The water is light blue, and the foam thrown up by the vessel, of a light red tint, while the sky presents a rich livid glow, more deep and rich as it approaches the horizon, exceeding any thing I have ever seen, and reminding me of that of an Italian sunset, as described by travelers. It is certainly one of the most beautiful phenomena that I ever beheld. The sailing fish, called by seamen the Portugese Man of War, is occasionally seen, spreading his tiny sails to the wind, and gliding smoothly over the waves.

FEB. 8TH. We have been crossing the Gulf Stream since last evening. At 12 M., Key West was discovered, from the mast-head. At 1 ½ saw the Light-house and some buildings at a distance. In the evening, to relieve the monotony, one of the passengers brought out a violin, which was something new in the way of music, and we presently had some of the light-footed cutting the pigeon-wing, before a crowd of delighted spectators. At 9 ½ saw the Tortugas light, gleaming at a distance.

FEB. 9TH. The sun rose brightly. We have been making only two or three knots an hour, during the past night. At 10 A.M., a meeting of the company was called to elect officers. The following was the result: for

President,
CAPT. HARDING.

Vice- President,
CHARLES BRIGGS.

Secretary,
A. B. CLARKE

Directors,

B. F. BARKER,   E. W. BURKE,
JOHN H. HOLLIS,   ORA HOLTON,
—BROOKS.[1]

Treasurer,
DOCT.—ROBINSON[2]

In the evening, for our amusement, we had music, and an exhibition of feats of agility, on deck.

FEB. 10TH. As 12 o'clock, M. in lat. 25° 11', long. 85, Gulf of Mexico. The weather is uncomfortably warm. In the afternoon, a large number of dog-fish, from four to six feet long, were seen plunging about the vessel. Several men attempted to shoot them, but none were killed.

FEB. 12TH. At 1 o'clock at night a strong wind set in, called a norther. This wind is peculiar to the Gulf and vicinity, and sometimes blows violently for several days, from the north. The sea was very rough, and the consequence was, many on board were again sick. Nothing on board fit for a sick dog.

FEB. 13TH. The wind abated during the night, leaving a heavy swell. I took some breakfast, having eaten nothing since day before yesterday. At noon we were 345 miles from Brazos. In the evening a fine breeze sprang up.

FEB. 14TH. All engaged in putting their fire-arms in order, &c. A beautiful little fish, about six inches long, with stripes around its body, called the pilot fish, was observed following the rudder of the vessel most of the day. It is said to be a precursor of sharks. At 12 o'clock, M. lat 25° 26', long. 94° 46'.

FEB. 15TH. At 9 o'clock, A.M., we were supposed to be within 25 or 20 miles of Brazos. All were highly delighted with the expectation of soon seeing land. At 10 o'clock a storm was seen rapidly approaching from the north. All sail were immediately taken in. The first gust passed by, just ahead of us; the second bore directly down upon us. We took to our berths, and were tossed about under a double reefed sail, with the helm lashed down, all night.

FEB. 16TH. The wind continued to rage. It was attended with a greater degree of cold than we had experienced since leaving N.Y. Was not able to leave my berth.

FEB. 17TH. After sunrise, the wind gradually abated. At 9 o'clock we had one sail hoisted. We were now supposed to be about fifty miles south of Brazos. At noon, a large school of dolphins were gamboling about the vessel; they kept along with us for sometime. At 3 P.M., land was seen from the mast. Kept off during the night.

FEB. 18TH. In the morning we came up, off Brazos, but the wind and waves were so high that we were obliged to keep away from shore. This is a dangerous coast, and many vessels have been lost here. There is a dangerous bar before the place, and only small craft can pass it in good weather; but when it is rough, it is dangerous for any steamboat, or vessel. We consequently cruised back and forth by Brazos all day, with a high sea.

FEB. 19TH. The steamboat not yet being able to come to our relief, we continued to cruise about, a part of the time in sight of land, constantly fearing that we might again be driven off at a distance.

FEB. 20TH. We came to anchor, about five miles off Brazos Santiago. Capt. Summer was taken on shore by a government steamer, and returned late in the afternoon. We cannot be taken off before tomorrow, as all the private steamers are away, and those of the government busy.

FEB. 21ST. The morning bright. Our baggage was brought on deck early, to be in readiness. All eyes were then anxiously turned towards the shore for the boat. It arrived at 10, when our goods were taken on board by means of the small boats. Arriving at 12, I immediately sought Major Chapman, U.S. Quartermaster, to whom I had a letter of introduction. He invited some of the Westfield men to his house, where we saw his wife, who is from Westfield, and with whom I had some acquaintance. Brazos Santiago, so famous during the Mexican war, as our military depot, is situated on a bank of sand. It is now a military station, and with the exception of the government buildings, consists principally of miserable shanties. An old steamboat is hauled up on the sand, and is used for a hotel, post- office, &c. I here first saw specimens of the Mexican, or "blanket race." I noticed some small companies sitting on the ground playing at monte, and other favorite games of chance, and passing the "pesos" freely. The Mexicans are a gambling nation, but they are said to engage in it more for the excitement than otherwise; hence you will never hear them express themselves in so extravagent terms at a gain or loss, as the Americans, who play for the money. Through the influence of Major Chapman, we procured passage for Brownsville, in a government boat. We left Brazos at 3 P.M. At the mouth of the Rio Grande we took a schooner in tow, to conduct it across the bar, which is a dangerous one. Several miles before entering the mouth of the Rio Grande, I noticed the line of its muddy waters, before it is blended with those of the blue sea. At a miserable village here, lie half a dozen government steamboats which were used in the war. They are now for sale.

February 22 — March 17, 1849

FEB. 22D. We passed Palo Alto in the night. It consists of but a few huts. I was waked early in the morning by the music of multitudes of birds, that were singing their wild and strange notes in the chapparal along the banks. At sunrise we saw a wolf leaving the Mexican side, where he had probably been committing depredations, endeavoring to cross to the chapparal in Texas. He kept on until he had got within three rods of the bow of the boat, when he turned to go back. Some of our men fired at him but he escaped safely to the shore. A few miles below Brownsville, where we stopped to wood, some of us called at a rancho, where we saw a Mexican shoe-making. The houses were made of reeds, sticks, and mud, not as good as the negro cabins of the southern states. There was no furniture of any value. In one of the shanties some women were making bread on a board which they held in their laps. While passing up the river we observed the men on the Mexican side engaged in ploughing the fields, as soon as it was light. They commence their labors thus early in the day to avoid the intense heat of the sun. Their farming utensils are of the simplest kinds. The plough is like that used by the ancient Jews, and other primitive people, being simply a crooked stock, or fork of a tree, one branch of which serves for the handle, another for the beam, while a prong answers for a share, without the aid of iron. The yokes are straight poles, lashed to the horns of the oxen by thongs; and in the place of whips they use poles or goads, with one end sharpened, with which they pierce the cattle unmercifully. Arriving at Brownsville, we learned that the cholera had just broken out there.

FEB. 23D. Last night two or three died of the cholera. One was a man who danced at a fandango till late at night.[1] Called on Dr.

Clarke's trail through Mexico

Jarvis, surgeon of the army; he gave some information in regard to the proper medicines and treatment of the cholera. Some of our company went over the Matamoras, one mile distant, and called on the American consul. We procured forty-five passports for the company. Our consul asked $2 for the certificates, and the alcalde $1 for the passports, making $3 for each person. To get the alcalde to sign our passports, we were directed to a grog shop, where we were told that he could generally be found; and where we did find him. Oranges were ripe in the gardens. Looked in at a boys' school. The boys were repeating in concert, and made as much noise as a flock of blackbirds. They appeared cheerful enough. The town contains eight or ten thousand inhabitants. There are long blocks of buildings, generally one story high, presenting a face of bare wall, with but few windows; the front wall extending above the roof, so as to hide it from sight. Like most Mexican towns, with the exception of the plaza, it has more the appearance of a large brick-kiln, ready for burning, than any thing else to which I can compare it. The cottages in the suburbs are built of reeds, some of the poorer sort very open, and thatched with palm leaf. One thing that first attracts the attention of a stranger, is the great number of grog-shops. Those of the first class are fitted up in the most expensive and attractive style, the shelves being well filled with bottles of aguardiente, (native brandy,) mescal, wines, &c. The different grades are well patronized, and are the lounging places of all classes. Took dinner at a Mexican eating-house, and for the first time, ate their tortillas, their universal bread at meals. In the centre of the Plaza is a square, set out with shrubs and flowers. I was informed that it was the work of American soldiers. Eight persons were buried in Brownsville who died of cholera, yesterday.[2]

FEB. 24TH. In the afternoon we left in a steamboat for Camargo. At the time of our leaving, fifteen deaths were reported for the day, and nine died of the cholera last night. Great numbers are sick at the hospitals. In passing up the river, we saw several California companies, encamped on its banks. Two boats arrived yesterday with one hundred each. We proceeded till 11 o'clock at night, when we ran to the shore and waited till morning.

FEB. 25TH. Passed three yokes of oxen, mired in the river. They are not unfrequently seen in that condition. They go down to drink and become mired in the quicksand. It costs the indolent Mexicans more to get them out, than they are worth. So they are left to perish, and become prey to the buzzards and ravens. I observed a quantity of geese eggs floating down the river. I was mentioning it to a friend, who declared that he had already seen several thousands. We afterwards saw large numbers. Not far above, was a sand bar, just above the surface of the water, almost white with them, and every wave was washing them off. Large flocks of geese were occasionally passed, some of them containing more than one hundred. They pair off in May, and go north. Turkies are very plenty; the captain of our boat said that on his last trip up the river, they killed twenty-one at the stopping places at night. The wood used by the boats, is ebony and mesquite; they now pay only $1.50 per cord; it formerly cost $2.50. Prickly pears are used for feeding cattle, in the absence of grass. It is thrown into the fire and the prickles burnt off, when it makes excellent feed. Some of the plants weigh one or two hundred pounds, and are eight or ten feet high.

FEB. 26TH. This morning, on stopping to wood, several men imprudently went out a short distance for game. Shepherd and Green, members of our company, became bewildered in the chapparal, although when the boat started, they were within a few rods of it. The boat passed up the river about a mile, when the captain at last concluded to stop. They then rang the bell, and several men went in search of them. When found, they were wet with the heavy dew from the bushes, ready to faint from fatigue, and almost wild with desperation. They had become entangled in the bushes and thought they had traveled several miles; to comfort them, they were told that the thicket was the nest of a desperate band of robbers. They had killed one turkey. The captain was highly censured for leaving them. At noon passed the Mexican town, Reynosa, of two or three thousand inhabitants. An American deserter, from camp Ringold, was brought on board here by the Mexicans. As this was a government boat, several officers were on board, and he was taken in custody. On stopping to wood, a few miles above, some of us visited a rancho at a short distance, and with the aid of the little Spanish that we had learned, inquired the price of some wild horses that were in a corral. We here first saw the Mexican dexterity in lassooing them. Large flocks of pelicans were seen in the river.

FEB. 27TH. Last night Mr. James Pond, one of the passengers, from Utica, N.Y., died of the cholera. He was on deck in the afternoon, but complained of being unwell, and went to his berth. At dusk I learned that he was better. At midnight I was waked by one of the company announcing his death. It struck a chill over the passengers, who were now sure that although they had escaped from Brownsville, yet we now had the cholera, in its most violent form among us. Mr. Pond was a man of remarkable fluency of speech, had become acquainted in all parts of the world, was known to all on board, and had contributed a large share to their entertainment. He was buried at half-past one on the Mexican shore, where a cross was erected to indicate his grave. A little before his death a member of our company discovered that he was a freemason, and as there were several of that order on board, they took charge of him, and performed for him the last sad offices of duty. Three more cases of cholera today. At 4 P.M., we landed six miles below Camargo. The boat went on to the military station, called Davis' Rancho. We camped for the first time, and kept a guard at night, on the bank of the river.

FEB. 28TH. We hired two ox-teams of a Scotchman to convey our goods to Camargo. We had barrels of bread, pork, and other provisions, besides tools, and tents, which were more cumbersome to us than the "impedimenta" to an old Roman army. In the first place they were to be carried up a very steep bank to the wagons. Then with miserably poor oxen, that had for yokes, poles lashed to their horns, and were driven at a snail pace, although cruelly mauled with goads of the size of bean poles, across a sand plain, under a broiling sun,—we arrived at Camargo. We passed, on the road, hundreds of graves of American soldiers, who fell a prey to disease at this place. On arriving at Camargo, it was with great difficulty that we could get the teams into the ferry boat, to cross the Rio San Juan; we however got everything over and camped, at dark, in the American fort, used by Gen. Taylor as a place of retreat, in case of a defeat, while engaged farther up in the country, on the west bank of the river, opposite the town. This fort covers several acres, and is formed by strong embankments of earth. The second of the three dogs brought by the passengers from N.Y., in crossing the sand plain to-day, exhibited symptoms of madness, or something resembling it. Like the first, which was thrown overboard at Brazos, he would dash about and run against any object that happened to be in the way; but when brought to his senses, he endeavored to make amends for his conduct to his friends, as if conscious of his extravagant behavior. We were very sorry to lose him, as he was a fine animal. We attributed it to the sudden change of climate, or perhaps to the effects of confinement on the vessel. The scenery along the Rio Grande is of the beautiful order, with ranchos interspersed at intervals, on the Mexican side. The banks are from ten to fifteen or twenty feet high, the water very muddy, and the current from three to four miles per hour. This river is perhaps the most important one in Mexico. Like the Nile, it receives no tributaries of importance for several hundred miles from its mouth, and consequently is nearly the same size for the distance.

MARCH 1ST. The dogs kept up a constant yelping, in Camargo, all night,—which mingled with the braying of donkeys, and the occasional howling of packs of wolves, near the camp, composed our serenade. Several persons are sick with the cholera. At 10½ o'clock, Green and myself went down to the rancho, near our landing, on the Rio Grande, where several of the sick were left yesterday. I was commissioned to receive the funds from Dr. Robinson, the treasurer, who was sick. The heat of the sun was very oppressive. Found Parsons very sick, and Whittemore still worse.

MARCH 2ND. At one o'clock at night, it being the most favorable time, the sick from the rancho were brought in, and a camp pitched for them a little out of the fort, where the dust was less disagreeable. In the morning, Dr. Robinson, Whittemore, Parsons and Kircher, were very sick, Stone and others complaining. Went over to Camargo, by direction of Dr. Scott of Miss., to procure medicine of Dr. Smith, the American physician. The remainder of the day I attended on Dr. Robinson. Our situation at this place is extremely uncomfortable. With a scorching sun, a constant south wind, hot and unwholesome, raising the dust, which is very fine, about the old fort, covering the baggage, and even entering our mouths and eyes. This, of itself, is enough to create a pestilence. Add to this, the pestilence is in the camp. Half a dozen are sick with the cholera, while others are frightened at what they fear to be symptoms of its approach. Many a poor American soldier found his grave here.

MARCH 4TH. Kircher died this morning. He was decently buried in a coffin, a little out of the fort.

At a meeting held to-day, it was voted to divide the company into three divisions, and divide the property of the original company into three parts, apportioning a share to each. The physicians advise us to leave the place, as it is very unhealthy, and we voted to do so, after making suitable provisions for the sick, who may not be able to go with us. There are also in the Fort, a Mississippi and Connecticut company, who have the cholera among them.

The committee appointed for the purpose have made arrangements with Dr. Smith to take charge of the sick at his house, provide the attendance of a servant, &c., for $4.00 per day, for which funds were appropriated by the company, before dividing. Dr. Robinson, Whittemore, and Parsons remain, with some of their friends to take care of them.

MARCH 5TH. In the morning all were engaged in making

preparations to leave, and anxious to be off. Our division had purchased a government wagon and four mules at Camargo, to carry our baggage. Loading our wagon with baggage, we placed the zink [zinc] boat at the top, under cover, in which Briggs, who is sick, rode quite comfortably. The thermometer is probably at 100°. Leaving the fort at 11 o'clock, we traveled twelve miles to a rancho, and encamped for the night.

MARCH 6TH. Our company rose early and having breakfasted before light, were on our march at a proper hour. We had gone but a mile, when one of the mules fell in the road. After working over him an hour, we succeeded in getting him on his legs. The road, a part of the way to-day, was extremely rough, frequently crossed by deep aroyas [arroyos] and gulleys. Coming to a little bank, at the edge of some hills, in the heat of the day, we discovered a small spring issuing from the mud, the first we had seen in the country. It was most acceptable to us. We crossed the beds of what in the rainy season are large rivers, 15 or 20 feet deep. We were obliged to-day, frequently to put our shoulders to the wheels, and not only that, but push the wagon up long hills. We arrived at Mier before night, worn down with fatigue, thinking it a slow and laborious method of getting to California.[3] Mier is a dirty place, containing a few thousand inhabitants. It is situated on a small river that empties into the Rio Grande. On the plaza was a battle in the Texan war, in which the Mexicans did much execution, being defended by the parapets on the buildings which surround them. We met with a number of Americans here; they are generally deserters, gamblers, traders, and smugglers, with occasionally one that has settled in the country.[4]

In this place there are several billiard rooms which do not seem to want for customers. The passion for gambling is so great, that it is not uncommon to see small groups collected in some shady place, seated upon the ground, engaged in their favorite game of cards, called "Monte." But few of the inhabitants seem to be working at any trade, and it is difficult to conceive how the Mexicans generally get a living.

When the women are seen doing any thing, it is either making tortillas, or washing at the river. Almost any time in the day several dozen may be found at the river washing, and although not remarkably neat in some of their habits, they certainly deserve to have the credit of keeping their clothing (much of which is white,) very clean. The children are but little expense as to clothing before they are six or eight years old, as a large proportion of both sexes may be observed in all the villages, up to this age, in a state of perfect nudity.

Another division of the company arrived in the evening.

MARCH 7TH. We thought it best to dispose of our heavy baggage and wagon and purchase riding mules, and pack the company's animals with what provisions were necessary.[5] We sold our boat and many of our tools, but tried to carry some along. Two of the N. Adams company visited our camp. They had a division today. All prudent men are willing to get clear of the joint stock companies after a fair trial. At 10 P.M., Sam, our interpreter, Foot, and a young American who professed a very extensive acquaintance about here, started up the river, 30 miles, to purchase mules for the company.

MARCH 8TH. The men arrived with the mules, late at night. Visited Maynard and Cogswell who were left behind sick by the Connecticut company. Cogswell concluded to go on with us.

MARCH 9TH. The mules were divided among the company. After some of the best were rated at a few dollars premium, and those had purchased them that thought they were able, the remainder were drawn by lot. The consequence was, as many of the mules were broken-down pack animals, in a miserable condition, some of the company found themselves poorly mounted.

MARCH 10TH. Our "nice young American" who assisted in purchasing the mules, came into camp with two or three of his associates, with their pistols, and demanded about $60 for his services yesterday. As some of us objected to the amount, he wished us to recollect that we were not now at home, prices were different from the States, perhaps we had never traveled out of our own country before, &c. A certain sum was named by the company which he was given to understand he might receive, or refuse as he thought proper. He concluded to accept it, as we did not appear to be frightened by him or his companions, and they observed that we also had a few pistols.

MARCH 11TH. After much vexation and delay in packing our mules, which was a kind of business entirely new to us, we got under way. Some of the riding mules not having been trained to it, started for the chapparal, and could not be made to stop, until they had landed their riders among the rocks and brush.

We find it necessary to have a care for each other, and see that none fall behind, or serious accidents might often occur. As our journey to-day was without water, several members suffer from the heat of the sun, which was about 100°.

I found a man in the afternoon who had, unnoticed, fallen behind a company before us, laying in the chapparal, his mule tied near him, and unable, from exhaustion, to proceed. I fortunately had some cordials in my haversack, which I administered, and in a short time had the satisfaction of seeing him revive so as to be able to go along with us. A number of our company also came near being melted. Camped at Chicherona Creek. Distance six leagues.

MARCH 12TH. Starting early, we arrived at Ponta Guda [Punta Aguda] at 11 A.M., where we found water and a little green grass. Here the Americans, in the time of the war, burned a small village to drive out the Guerillas. We met with a Hartford company at that place. Going on, in the afternoon, we were overtaken by a most violent storm. Night coming on, with an occasional sprinkle or rain, we found it difficult to make our way. As we were passing along in the darkness, a gun was fired from the chapparal, and the ball passed just over the heads of some of the men.

We arrived at Seralvo [Cerralvo] between 9 and 10 at night, and with difficulty found a place to camp in the darkness. However, we pitched down, without ceremony, on a grassy yard before a house, and were plentifully supplied with eggs, milk, &c. Distance 30 miles.

MARCH 13TH. Went a few miles and camped early near a burnt and deserted village. A Mexican boy brought in a plenty of goat's milk.

MARCH 14TH. Started at 4 A.M., and after a good day's travel, camped at Rhamos. We killed a few birds for supper. On our way we passed the skeletons of the wagoners, who were killed by the guerilla Urrea [Urrera].

MARCH 15TH. About sunrise we passed through Marin, a neat looking place, situated on high grounds, with a valley surrounding it, and the Sierra Madra mountains in the distance. As the sun rose upon the steep rocks of the mountains, they exhibited in places the appearance of glowing coals of fire. Camped at San Domingo, near Walnut Springs, Taylor's old camping ground, six miles from Monterey [Monterrey].

MARCH 16TH. While loading our pack mules I noticed a woman coming from a neighboring house, and seeing a large hatchet, which belonged to one of the company, lying upon the ground, I cautioned the owner to see that she did not steal it. In two or three minutes afterward, the hatchet was gone, and the woman seen walking rapidly towards her house. We made a sally after her, and just as she reached the house overtook her, but could find nothing of the missing article. How she could have stowed it about her person, we did not take measures to ascertain. This circumstance at least convinces us that the Mexicans can steal while we are looking at them.

We drove into Monterey, passing through town, and camped near the Bishop's Palace, about a mile out. Everything looks green, from the showers which they have had here among the mountains, while the low grounds through which we have passed is parched up.

MARCH 17TH. Monterey, the capital of the State of New Leon, containing 13,000 inhabitants, is situated on a large plain which is partly surrounded by the Sierra Madra mountains, perhaps 3 or 4 miles distant. These mountains are said to be nearly 2 miles high above the level of the sea. Some of them are very pointed, and worn into various fantastic shapes by the action of rains, and deeply furrowed on the sides. They form a very singular and striking picture in the scenery. There is a story that Gen. Taylor wished to see the American flag planted on the top of one of the highest peaks, and offered $300 to anyone who would accomplish it. That it was attempted by two men, who spent two days in fruitless endeavors and abandoned it. I will not vouch for the truth of the story.

I visited the Bishop's Palace which was garrisoned by the Mexicans and taken by Gen. Worth. It is situated on a hill, a mile from the city; it overlooks the city, and the whole valley, which is very beautiful and susceptible of irrigation. It reminds one of the baronial castles of Europe. Its inside is torn out, and there are some holes made by cannon balls, also some remains of paintings left on the walls. In front is a small fort, apparently built for the occasion. In the centre is a cistern, made like a well, about 20 feet in diameter, and neatly plastered with hard cement. The water from the roof was probably conducted into it. The road to it is by a zigzag ascent, up the steep side of the hill. The view from it is very splendid, the town lying beneath, green with orange, lemon, fig, and other trees. There are a number of American merchants here, an apothecary and physicians, and it is visited by traders from the States. The buildings being composed of adobes with thick walls, formed in continuous blocks on each side of the streets, having parapets of the same material on the flat mud roofs, next to the streets, form excellent defenses, but inferior to forts, and it is not strange that the Americans had some hard fighting and were obliged to shed their blood freely, to drive them from these shelters.

The fortress is one of the most important in Mexico, and is still kept up. That at the city of Mexico has been abandoned.

The soldiers not on duty were out about the government buildings. We could not avoid noticing their inferior size and bearing to our American men; and our Yankees were generally of the opinion that each could whip two or three of them. Soon two of them commenced fighting with long knives, which all Mexicans carry, and in the use of which they excel, until one of them broke his knife on the other, when they were arrested by an officer, who seemed greatly enraged that they should exhibit such conduct in our presence. Many of the regular soldiers are said to be convicts for petty offenses, and are altogether an inferior shabby looking set, and appear to be roughly used.[6]

Our little company have today made a final division of all their provisions and other property. One mule that cost $30 sold for $20 ½. Another which cost $25 sold for $12 ½, making a sacrifice on nearly everything. Most of us were heartily glad to get rid of all company property. Another division arrived with Shepherd, (who had been severely injured by being thrown from a horse,) and Brooks, of whom I have not before heard, since leaving New York. I did not have an opportunity to see them.

March 18–April 15, 1849

MARCH 18TH. Leaving Monterey we traveled through a level valley [probably Rinconada Pass], between precipitous, parallel mountains, perhaps a mile high. The atmosphere is so clear, that we are often deceived in regard to distances. We camped at a rancho, where there was a stone wall from mountain to mountain. The roadside was set out with rows of cottonwood and century plants. Distance 30 miles.

MARCH 19TH. We ascended a mountain, early, at the top of which is a fort, built by Gen. Ampudia after the battle of Monterey.[1] There being no water convenient, and finding it difficult to procure provisions, he was obliged to evacuate the place. It was a strong position. Camped at a rancho, near which is a cotton factory. Distance 30 miles.

MARCH 20TH. Entered Saltillo at 9 A.M., and stopped at a large establishment, which was used by Gen. Taylor as a hospital. Saltillo looks well; its streets radiate from the plaza, which contains a splendid fountain and cathedral. Its population is 20,000. There are said to be a number of bands of guerillas in the place, who are upheld by some of the principal citizens. This place is famous for the manufacture of serapes, or woolen blankets, which are worn by the men, throughout the whole country; they cost from $25 to $500, with fine colors exquisitely woven; the poorer classes wear cheaper ones. In the afternoon we went out three or four miles, and camped at the hacienda Buena Vista, at the end of the battleground.

MARCH 21ST. Starting at 4, we passed over the battleground early. Dr. Scott of Miss., procured an arm of a soldier with the muscles dried upon it from the field. Our road lay over a wide plain, and it was extremely dusty and disagreeable—camped at Redamiedios, a small village of huts; distance, eight leagues.

MARCH 22ND. At 2 P.M., we passed a creek, but not being correctly informed as to the next watering place, we kept on until 9 o'clock at night, and camped by the roadside without water. Distance 30 or 35 miles.

MARCH 23D. In the morning we went five miles to the hacienda Castanasla and procured refreshments. The main building is two or three hundred feet long. The granary is also large. In this section the buildings of the ranchos are large, with many tenements strongly built of adobes, to defend them against the Indians. In the afternoon we went on to another large rancho under the mountains and encamped. Distance 20 miles.

MARCH 24TH. Leaving camp at sunrise, we commenced a passage up the mountain, by a winding and steep mule path. Having arrived at the top, we found several miles of table land, arriving at the edge of which, we all, animals as well as men, involuntarily stopped to view the prospect before us. The descent appeared to us, from above, in places almost perpendicular, while below, a vast plain stretched away in the distance, with a lake at the further side; we at last, however, all got down safely with our mules. This way is several miles nearer than the wagon-road. Arriving at the plain and passing over a large tract laid out with sluices for irrigation, we arrived at the hacienda Vajo, four miles from Parras, before sundown, and encamped in a beautiful grassy place at the edge of the village, under some fig and apricot trees. Some of us were invited to a fandango on the occasion of a wedding. The dance was held in the yard of one of the houses near by,—they danced to the music of a guitar, and all appeared merry.

A young English gentleman from Parras rode into our camp today upon a fine mule, richly caparisoned, the saddle, bridle and other trappings, which abound in the Mexican accoutrements, being richly mounted with silver. His high truncated cone of a hat, with broad brim, short jacket, with red silk sash, and breeches open to the knees, showing the pure white flowing drawers beneath, proved the perfect dandy. He was as officious as such gentlemen generally are, and politely invited us to visit various places and enjoy ourselves the best we could according to Mexican custom.

MARCH 25TH. Visited Parras. A Hartford, Mississippi, and other companies are camped here. Called on Dr. Chapman, an Englishman, from whom we obtained some information. Parras and its neighboring plantations contain 17,000 inhabitants; the town itself perhaps one half that number. It is beautifully situated on the banks of a lake of the same name, in one of the principal fruit districts of Mexico. There is a large park, equal in beauty to any in the States, adorned with shade trees, walks, and stone seats; its elevation above the sea, according to Dr. Weslizenius, is 4987 feet. In the neighborhood there are made annually 225,000 gallons of wine, which is of a superior quality. The vineyards are handsomely walled in with adobes, with gates which are kept locked and rills of water are conducted through them in every direction. The hacienda Vajo contains several very large buildings for wine presses, distilleries of aguardiente, granaries, &c. There are several fine avenues of trees, laid out with fine taste, interspersed with rose bushes, in the streets, which are watered by proper conduits. One of them in the direction of Parras is a mile long, forming a most delightful promenade or drive.

MARCH 26TH. Again visited Parras. That the Mexicans are most accomplished thieves, we have had abundant proofs; nearly every American company have had goods and arms stolen, notwithstanding the most vigilant watch. A company stopping here, whose rooms are within a court, the only entrance to which is through a strong arched gateway in the wall, had several guns stolen from their quarters at different times.

A company behind us also had arms stolen several nights in succession, by a man who followed them, although they kept two men on the watch at a time. The last night of his depredations, he crept up a little gulley by the side of which they were camped, and stole two or three guns that were lying near the heads of their owners.

The nearest alcalde was applied to, who promptly despatched men in pursuit, and captured the thief and sent him after the company, telling them to punish him as they thought proper. They concluded to whip him, and each of the company from who he had stolen were allowed to give him a certain number of lashes. Several men used the whip according to appointment, without his minding it much, until a man from North Adams, Mass., being of a mild disposition, refused to add his quota. A gentleman from the South, who happened to understand the use of the weapon, and being not particularly scrupulous, seeing how the matter was likely to terminate, begged leave to supply his place, and laid on the allotted number with such alacrity and skill, that the offender was likely to remember it for a long time.

A number of Alabamians arrived to-day and gave us the following account. Their company, which was a small one, had employed a young American at Brownsville to act as their interpreter. When we were in that place he also tried to unite himself to our company in the same capacity, but not liking his appearance we at once rejected him. Their company had arrived one day's journey from Monterey and had camped at the same place that we had done before them. In the morning a young doctor, a member of the company, and the interpreter, went upon the side of a mountain, which rose above the camp, to look for game. In the course of a few hours the interpreter returned without the doctor. On being interrogated as to what had become of him, he replied that there was no doubt but that the Indians had killed him, as they lived in the mountains. During the next night he stole the best mule in the company, together with a brace of pistols, and made his escape. After waiting a day or two, for the purpose of looking for the doctor, they came on, satisfied in regard to his fate, as he was known to have money about him.

MARCH 27TH. We have been undetermined whether to go by way of Mazatlan, or the land route by Chihuahua, but hearing that the passage by Mazatlan is very high, and many persons waiting there, we have finally determined to go by the way of Chihuahua, although we expect to encounter many difficulties. Leaving hacienda Vajo at 7, we traveled over a dry desert country, without water, 30 miles to El Pozo, (the well) a strongly walled rancho. The water is obtained from the well by horse power. We were waked in the night by a large wild animal rushing through our camp, jumping over some of us, as we lay asleep, and causing some of our animals to break their lariats.

MARCH 28TH. Passed through a dry valley called the Bolson (pouch) of Mapimi, with mountains on either hand. Objects that appeared no more than a half mile distant, we sometimes found to be two or three miles. About noon we saw in the horizon what some declared to be a body of water; others were of a different opinion. I supposed it to be either Lake Cayman or a smaller one near it.

This extensive plain has been but little explored. The wild recesses of the interior are the safe hiding places of hordes of savage Indians. Although a portion of it is sandy, a part is low ground, and thought to be well adapted for the cultivation of rice. The location of this valley being elevated about 4000 feet above the level of the sea, the climate is delightful, and if it were not for its remote interior situation it would doubtless prove a favorable section for cultivation. It is traversed by the river Nasas which empties into Lake Cayman, and is more than 400 miles long, and rises in the western part of the State of Durango.

We camped a little off the road, at a deserted rancho, situated on a small river, probably the Parral. The inhabitants of the rancho were murdered by the Indians about a year since; for a day or two past we have seen numbers of deer. We have been traveling, thus far, without a leader, but thinking that our movements would be better regulated if all should act more in concert, (and as it is necessary to go in a compact body and keep up a guard at night), we concluded to choose some one of our number to act as captain of the company, and I had the honor of being chosen to fill this undesirable situation.

MARCH 29TH. At noon we stopped at the village of San Lorenzo, where we procured bread—hot from the oven, as we often have done—corn for our animals, &c. Bread of several kinds can be obtained in the principal towns. *Pan-arena* [harina] is flour bread, which they make in small loaves; *Pan-a-maiz* is corn bread; *Pan-dulce* is sweet bread; *Pan-manteca* shortened bread. The tortilla is universally used, especially out of villages where they have not the convenience of a mill to make flour. When corn is used, it is soaked in ley or lime water till it becomes soft. To grind it they use a *matate,* which consists of a stone about two feet long, standing on legs, the front ones the shortest to make it incline. The sides of the stone are raised, leaving a wide groove in the middle, into which the grain is put with one hand, and a stone fitting the groove is moved with the other, something as painters grind their paints. A rich paste is formed, sufficiently moist, which is patted between the hands very skillfully, tossing it up and catching it until it is made much thinner than a griddle cake. It is then thrown upon a flat stone or piece of iron which is very hot, over the fire, without being sprinkled with either flour or grease. One side is sufficiently baked in an instant, when it is turned, and in a few seconds it is ready for eating, and makes a very palatable and wholesome bread.

On starting in the afternoon, through the stupidity of our interpreter, we got upon the wrong road. We were met just before night by several mounted Mexicans, armed with muskets and lances. One of them returned and offered to show us the public road, which he represented as being but a short distance. Darkness coming on, and some of the men suspecting an ambuscade or other foul play, I ordered two riflemen ahead with our Mexican, with orders to keep a strict watch over him. We went on through the chapparal till 8 o'clock, when coming to an opening we camped, keeping our guide under guard.

MARCH 30TH. Passing through the village of El Emetre in the

morning, we were not favorably impressed with the appearance of some of the men, who were stirring about in a suspicious manner. In these little inland towns are many banditti, and it is necessary to go well armed. Guns were fired when we left the village—the land to-day was excellent, interspersed with large cotton-woods. We also for the first time passed through tracks of cane-brake. In the afternoon we watered at a small muddy pond; the mules being very thirsty, made a rush for the water. One riding mule that happened to be loose, ran under a limb and tore off his saddle and baggage which fell into the mud and water. A pack mule with his load fell in the middle of the mud-hole, and was with great difficulty lifted out with poles. Others were in circumstances more or less melancholy. Some of the men were somewhat irritated at these misfortunes; others were calm and pleasant though in the mud up to their middles; it was a rare and interesting sight. At last the mules were all got out, the thickest of the mud scraped off from the baggage, and we went on a few miles and camped in a plain of fine grass. Distance 30 miles.

MARCH 31ST. We left camp at sunrise. The men killed a small beef which we found on the plain, as we had been informed that we could probably obtain no food for a considerable distance ahead. We watered at a well, one and a half miles farther on, where to our surprise we found inhabitants.

Between a notch in the mountain and Mapimi, we counted ten or twelve crosses, which are erected where persons have been murdered;—encamped at Mapimi. There are at this place furnaces for smelting the ore of copper, silver and gold, which is obtained from the neighboring mountains. The cinders have formed extensive hillocks in the suburbs of the town. Distance 32 miles.

APRIL 1ST. We spent the day in camp at Mapimi; we were visited by many Mexicans; some of them are anxious to go to California. One of them insisted, for a long time, that he would go as my peon. A Dutchman who was managing a furnace spent part of the day with us. Also a negro, formerly from Missouri, who appeared among the first with this blanket race. The Alcalde paid us a visit and invited me to take supper with him, but rather unfortunately I did not understand the invitation until too late to accept it.

APRIL 2D. Leaving Mapimi, we passed over a plain, then through a notch of a mountain, where we picked up several specimens of copper ore in our path, and arrived at Carana, a large rancho strongly walled in and defended by two brass cannon. There are here a copper furnace and a distillery for making mescal. Mescal is an aromatic kind of spirituous liquor, made from maguey or agave Americana, a species of aloe similar to that which grows in Spain, the leaves of which are six or eight feet long. A mild fermented liquor called pulque, much esteemed among the natives, and which is considered by them a panacea for many diseases, is made from the same plant. A good plant will yield from one to two gallons per day. It is collected in a hollow, cutting out the heart of the trunk into which the sap oozes; it continues to run for two or three months, and the produce of each plant per day, is worth about one real, or 12 ½ cents. Although it grows wild in nearly all parts of Mexico, its cultivation is very profitable.

Three Americans on their way down the country from Chihuahua visited our camp; they were of a certain class who roam over this country. They told some wonderful stories of the danger of Indians on our road. Questioning one of them in regard to some places he professed to have visited in California, I found that he knew nothing about them, and often contradicted himself. Finally, one of them becoming pretty familiar with some of the men, advised them to look out for one of his comrades, as he would steal if he had a chance. They were given to understand that their company was not desirable in camp at night. Distance eight miles.

APRIL 3D. In crossing the mountains, we picked up some ores. In the afternoon Sam, Hollis, and Cogswell fell behind. We camped in a valley and looked anxiously for the rear, as we were in a by-path among the wild mountains, and we saw signs of Indians. Morris came up and camped with us. Frost was seen in the morning.

APRIL 4TH. Thinking that the missing had taken a path to the right, we went on by a mule path to La Sarca [La Zarca], three leagues. While at this place, a boy running near one of our mules was kicked senseless by him. We carried him to one of the rooms within the walls, and by using proper means, soon had the pleasure of reviving him. The inhabitants had filled the room in the excitement of the moment, anxious to learn the extent of the injury; the bell of the chapel happening to ring for 12 o'clock, the hour of prayer, it was interesting to see the crowd of rough men, in such circumstances, in obedience to their religious customs, instantly pull off their hats, and stand a few minutes uncovered, in silence.

We waited until 3 P.M., when we learned from a Mexican that three Americans had arrived at Creusa the evening before, and left at 10 this morning for Cero Gordo [Cerro Gordo]. They had consequently taken a path to our right and were ahead; we therefore went on four leagues; and camped without water. This is a good grass country.

APRIL 5. Leaving camp early, we arrived at Cero Gordo at 1 P.M., where we found our lost men who had taken a nearer path among the mountains. A Spaniard with nine wagons, loaded with loaf sugar, mescal, and other choice groceries, was camped here. He was going from Zacetecas to Chihuahua. Distance to Zacetecas 100 leagues; to Chihuahua, 67 leagues. About 200 soldiers are stationed here on the lookout for the Camanches, who are in the vicinity. We went out two leagues and camped on good grass. Some of the troops went out with a herd of horses to the grass at the same time. One of our wildest mules became frightened and got loose from his owner. Two or three of the dragoons volunteered their services and pursued him with their lassos, and being a fleet animal, it took nearly fifteen minutes to catch him. The ground was very rough, with many gulleys and hillocks, but the horses were allowed to take their own course, and followed him as a dog would in pursuit of game.

APRIL 6TH. We left camp at sunrise, and found water after

traveling two leagues. We stopped to refresh our animals at noon where there was a plenty of grass, and arrived at the rancho La Noria, at 3 P.M., nine leagues. We camped for the first time, in a corral, within the walls; the wind blew the dust and litter over us; the fleas annoyed us; the pigs broke into the enclosure several times during the night, so that with all our grievances, we procured but little sleep, and we were willing ever afterwards to camp in a clean place, away from all their filthy buildings, although obliged to keep up a guard. Many of the ranchos in the State of Chihuahua are built like forts, and may be considered as such. Their form is the following:—A strong adobe wall, in the form of a square, from 200 to 400 feet on a side, and 15 or 20 feet high. There is sometimes a small chapel at one corner, with its chime of bells; it has one strong gate in the centre of one side; the rooms for the proprietors are on each side of the entrance within. There are built against the walls on the inside a range of rooms for the peons; these have but one door which opens into the court. There are no windows and no chimneys, but a hole is left in one corner for the smoke to escape. There are no floors and no furniture, except a few earthen pots and occasionally a brass kettle for cooking; their beds are principally of ox hides and sheep skins; the roofs are of the height of the walls, nearly flat, and made by laying poles and twigs upon the rafters, upon which is laid a layer of mud or clay, nearly a foot thick, which becomes hard by being dried in the sun, and sheds the rain. Upon the tops of the roof sentinels are placed when Indians are in the neighborhood.

APRIL 7TH. Morris, who last night encamped in the court, in the morning missed three of his horses. Some of our company volunteering their assistance, seized several of the landlord's horses, and declared that they should not be given up until those that were missing were produced. After considerable parleying, one of the Mexicans started for the chapparal, and soon brought them in. He had probably driven them there, hoping that they would be left. Passed La-Florida, a handsome rancho, one building of which is five or six hundred feet long, having a portico with arches and columns. Camped at Conception, a hacienda, one building of which we judged to be nearly 1,000 feet long.

APRIL 8TH. We traveled to Alenda [Allende] in the morning, and camped under a long avenue of cottonwood trees. The place contains about 11,000 inhabitants, and is one of the neatest that I have seen in the country. I became acquainted with an American resident, whose name is Hix. Provisions are very cheap; a man can live for 25 cents a day in the interior of the country. Meat is never weighed, but sold by the piece.

The women appear better featured and better dressed than in most places. Pears, peaches and quinces are about one half grown. One of the company has seen an apple-tree here which is a great rarity. We had a striking exhibition of the superiority of Mexican horsemanship to that of the Americans, which although amusing to most of us, came near being the death of one. As a number of us were walking from camp into town, a Mexican with a splendid wild horse, was prancing along the street, and although the horse showed great spirit, he seemed held in very good subjection. Our interpreter who prided himself on his horsemanship, asked the privilege of riding him. He was no sooner seated, than the animal seeing whom he had to deal with, began to rear and jump, and becoming ungovernable, dashed against the high adobe wall of a garden. Our man thinking it a good opportunity to get clear, clung to the top of the wall; the horse ran from under him, and consequently left him dangling. Thus ended his first lesson.

APRIL 9TH. We stopped for dinner, near St. Cruz, a miserable village. In the afternoon went out a few miles and camped without water. Distance, eleven leagues.

APRIL 10TH. After traveling a few miles in the morning, we left the main road to water at the river. On leaving the water, Burke's horse got loose, and ran off into the chapparal; he went in pursuit with two Mexicans, who had been with us for a day or two past, and said that they were going to Chihuahua. They had shared in our meals, and some of the company had walked several miles, at times, that one of them might ride. Arnold had loaned one of them a thick coat, as his blanket was poor, and he had just recovered from sickness. After the horse was brought in, the Mexican was seen no more; probably the coat had tempted him to stay behind, as he was seen after the horse was found. At 10 o'clock a Mexican met us, riding at full gallop, and gave us to understand that 100 Camanches and 500 Apaches were just over the river, about a mile distant, but on further inquiry, I learned that he had seen a great dust over the river, and supposed it must arise from that number of Indians as they were in the vicinity. He then started off at full speed to spread the information; we kept on as usual, but saw no Indians. There are some predatory bands in the neighborhood, but as we go armed, they keep out of our way; the Mexicans live in constant fear. At 11, camped where there was some grass near the river, when Morris came up and gave us the following information.

Mr. Jno. Hollis had been a member of the Hampden Mining Company, but since its dissolution, had been first with Luce, and of late, part of the time with Morris, and part with us. When we left Alenda on Monday morning, he staid behind with Morris, who we understood was going to take a nearer road. It seems that he left, when we had got a mile or two on the road, and Morris soon after; when Morris had proceeded about two miles, he perceived a mule a little from the road, which he took to be Hollis', and on going to it, heard some one groaning. He found Hollis lying with his skull broken on the back of the head, and his face badly bruised. Two men were seen running at a distance, and were pursued by Morris and his Mexican attendant; they however ran along the side of a mountain, shouting, and made their escape towards town. Hollis was able to inform them in broken sentences, that a man had overtaken him, of whom he inquired if that was the road to Chihuahua. He pointed to a by-road and said that was the one. He knew better, and kept on; presently he felt something hit his head, when turning a little, he recollected seeing a man in the chapparal with a sling in his hand, just as he was falling from the mule. After taking part of his money and baggage they ran off.

Morris sent a messenger to Mr. Antonio Hix, the American gentleman who came out with the Alcalde and carried him to his house, in town, and promised to have him taken care of, and his money restored if possible, and should his health admit, to be sent on in some company that might follow. We went on and camped at a rancho called Rio Parral, near a river of that name. Not able to obtain much to eat.

APRIL I I TH. Leaving Rio Parral early, we arrived at the village of San Rosalie before noon. We here met with a party of twenty-eight from Texas, by the way of Corpus Christi and Monclova. They went without water three days at one time, lost one man who went to look for a mule, and suffered many hardships on this desert route. There is a garrison in this town. After procuring provisions, we proceeded about four leagues, searched for grass on the way. Having sent two men ahead, to select a place for a camp, they went on till dark without finding grass, and were obliged to camp without it.

APRIL 12TH. Leaving camp at 6 o'clock, in an hour we passed the village of La Cruz, where we stopped to give our animals grass. At 12 M., we arrived at Saucillo, situated on the river Conchos, now, in the dry season, about the size of the Chicopee. After we had stopped under the shade of the river bank, by the town, for two hours, and had procured corn for our animals as usual, we proceeded four or five miles, to some fine grass, where we camped. Sam and several others, stopped to kill a beef. I endeavored to dissuade them from it, but did not succeed. They shot at two young cattle, but did not kill either.

APRIL 13TH. The nights are very cool, which has been the case ever since we left Parras. After passing through a large meadow of grass, and crossing the river, which at times, from appearances, must convey a large stream of water, as the channel is wide and gravelly, and the banks high, we passed through San. Pablo, and camped on the other side, where there was plenty of grass. In the afternoon I visited the town, three quarters of a mile distant. Called on Mr. Favel, an American merchant from Virginia. San.

Pablo contains four thousand inhabitants; they are chiefly farmers. Coffee is fifty cents per pound; prints sell at about three times their value in the States. We looked into a church, where an old priest was counting his beads, and a dozen boys on their knees; we next visited a school. The boys were studying their lessons aloud; they were reading from catholic primers, printed at the city of Mexico. I saw an old volume of the dictionary of geography on the table; some of the boys were learning to write a coarse hand, and I saw one specimen of fine hand, similar to our old round hand, which was very good.

APRIL 14TH. We started from San. Pablo soon after sunrise, and passed over a large plain of low ground, covered with green grass, part of which had been burnt over, forming excellent feed. This grassy plain, extending for several miles on each side of San. Pablo, is as level as a floor, and supports large flocks of sheep and goats. We passed a small natural pond, upon which were large flocks of ducks. After going two miles, Sam discovered that he had left his ammunition, and returned, but could not find it. Stopped at the rancho Bachymber [Bachimba] to feed, at noon. When about to leave, Cogswell missed his only coat, a good cloth one, which had been stolen from his saddle. After threatening and storming for some time, he was obliged to give it up, as all the men about the rancho of course professed to know nothing about it. We then passed, by an old road, two leagues among the mountains, to a rancho, where there were some soldiers, but learning that there was another ahead, we went on and camped, where we found a little grass, at the foot of a sugar-loaf shaped mountain. Cogswell and Fowler ascended it, with considerable labor, as they found it much higher than it appeared from below. Some of the party killed a small beef, a Mexican gentleman from Chihuahua, in our company, recommending it. Distance eleven leagues.

APRIL 15TH. We left our camp in the mountains at half-past six. On our way, after arriving upon the plains, we saw a herd of thirteen deer. Arriving at Chihuahua at one P.M., we took off our packs by a spring, until we found a corral for our animals, and rooms for ourselves, which we did in the course of two hours. At four o'clock was a bull fight, which I determined to attend, as it was probably the only opportunity that would be presented in my life time, not only to gratify my curiosity, but to judge for myself the effect of such a spectacle, on a people who make it their chief amusement. The fight was in an amphitheatre, covering perhaps an acre of ground, built after the plan of those of the Romans. It is an octangular building of brick, with an arched covered gallery, at the circumference, with settees for the spectators. These are the best seats; below these are several ranges of stone seats, one above another, and still lower, on the ground, is an aisle, between which and the show ground, is a strong close fence of plank, seven or eight feet high. Within the fence is the arena, which covers a considerable space of ground. On one side are wide folding-doors, with a passage which leads under the seats, to a court behind, from which the animals are let into the arena.

The exercises commenced by one of the performers who was painted, and acted the part of a clown; he addressed the audience for about ten minutes. A good band of music was in attendance, which played at intervals, during the whole of the performance. A bull was then let into the arena. There were several footmen dressed in fancy style, and four horsemen;—the footmen with scarlet and yellow mantles, of light stuff, which they shook before the animal to enrage him, and to blind him when he came at them. They carried their mantles suspended upon their swords; they also had short javelins, adorned with large festoons of ribbons, which they darted or thrust into him, as they dexterously ran past; also very large rosetts of ribbon fastened to barbs which they aimed to stick on his forehead. When the bull made an attempt upon the horsemen, they generally caught him in the shoulder with their spears. After considerable loss of blood, the footmen approached, and endeavored to pierce him with their swords, over his horns, which he did not allow, but finally being fatigued, he lay down for a moment, when he was struck one blow on the neck, with a strong knife, which severed the spinal cord, and killed him. A pair of mules, richly harnessed, and with bells, were then galloped in, and he was dragged out by one foot in an instant. Time twenty minutes. The second animal was more furious than the first. He was finally killed by a stroke of the sword, back of the horns.

The third bull was very wild. His attention was attracted for sometime by the mantles. The footmen when closely pursued, as they frequently were, fled and leaped upon or over the fence, before which there was a narrow step to assist them in mounting. He presently ran at a horse and gored him badly in the breast, and soon after another, in the haunches. He then made several attempts to follow the footmen, who worried him sadly, over the barrier, and at length succeeded in striking one of them as he had reached the top of the fence. He then pursued another closely across the ground, and, to our astonishment, succeeded in leaping the fence after him, into the aisle. A number of our men say the fence was eight feet high. He was driven around and again brought into the arena. He was soon after thrust through with a sword behind the shoulders. Still, he was as dangerous as ever, but they at length succeeded in drawing the sword, and he was killed by a blow from the same instrument. Time twenty minutes. A wild horse was then let in, lassooed and rode in the ring.

The fourth bull was lassooed and thrown, and a rope made fast around his body. A man, who I understood was a convict, then mounted him; he was then allowed to get up, when he commenced plunging and jumping, and at last succeeded in throwing him to the ground. He then tossed him, gored him with his horns, and trampled on him most furiously, until his attention was called away by the footmen, when the man was dragged out apparently lifeless, and I soon after learned that he was dead. He then, more furious from his success, made a plunge at a horseman, threw the horse against the barrier and gored him in the side until his entrails dragged upon the ground. The rider made his escape. The horse was dragged out—great applause. He was finally pierced with the sword until he reeled from loss of blood, when he was felled by a single blow, amidst the applause of the ladies.

The fifth bull made a charge upon a horse until he was disabled, his horns entering his haunches, about half their length. He then ran in every direction, as if trying to find some place of escape, then stopped short and looked wildly around at the spectators, who were applauding in their seats. He then made at another horse, threw him against the barrier, tore him in a shocking manner. The rider could not keep him off with his spear, and with much difficulty made his escape. A man then ran past, and stuck a short spear armed with fire works into his shoulder, which soon exploded, and the combustible burst in his flesh. he was worried and tormented until he ran and bellowed furiously, and was finally dispatched amidst the plaudits of the spectators. The sixth bull was let into the ring for the amusement of the Greisers.[2] About fifty men and boys showed their dexterity in avoiding him. He at length got one of them down, but he fortunately escaped without much injury.

The whole performance filled me with disgust, such as I had never before experienced. A people that delight in such cruel performances, must naturally be fit candidates for robbers and assassins. But what is the most surprising is, that the ladies, to whom are attributed the finer feelings of nature, should, in this enlightened age, countenance such spectacles with their presence and approbation. Ladies, many of them of Castilian blood, with fair complexions, regular features, and superbly dressed, crowded the upper seats. There were, probably, three thousand persons present, and the amphitheatre would contain as many more.

April 16–29, 1849

APRIL 16TH. This morning I obtained in the market a bowl of chocolate, very rich, for one quartillo, about three cents, and a dish of tripe and parched corn, for the same. Before dinner, I called on the prefector, and showed my passport, and gave notice to the company to do the same. In the afternoon I called on some American merchants in order to obtain information concerning the road to California. Graham's and Cook's [Cooke's] route is the one recommended, but the fact is, little is known of the way, or the difficulties. There is a nearer route, through the mountains, which is said to be rough and dangerous.

APRIL 17TH. We spent the day in visiting the town, and making preparations for our journey. In the afternoon I walked about town with Burke; visited the ruins of an old cathedral, which were magnificent. Troops were out drilling, they were recruits, to proceed against the Indians. Their martial music is wild and shrill. The women of the wealthier classes are expensive in their dress; this consists in part of a skirt of white, or other light stuff, or silk, well supplied with flounces. The head is covered with the *roboso* [*rebozo*], a long scarf, going over the top of the head and crossing on the breast. In their manners they are easy and graceful, and always appear with a certain air of native grace and self-possession, which is apt to impress a stranger favorably. They appear in the streets more commonly than in the States. Some of them keep little shops, and others have stands in the public squares for the sale of fruits, pastry, confectionery, &c., while others keep fires in the market places, where they cook and sell their various dishes. A person can get a pretty good meal for six cents, and many of the inhabitants sometimes take their meals at these places.

The greater part of the Mexican ladies have a complexion too dark to accord with our ideas of beauty, but the descendants of the Castilians, who are more numerous in the large towns, may well dispute the palm with the Anglo Saxon race. Their beauty is of the most fascinating kind. Large deep black eyes, shaded with long lashes, glossy raven hair, which they arrange with good taste; complexions coming nearer to the brunette than any other which we have among us, and almost universally contrast well with a fine set of teeth.

We saw but few carriages; they are rich, but heavy, and drawn by mules, and attended by servants. The corral where we stopped was owned by a French lady, who lived in one part of the building. She was an intelligent woman, having been educated in her youth in Philadelphia, and spoke several languages fluently. She had with her two daughters, who were interesting young ladies. The situation was in the highest part of the town, with lines of cottonwoods in the streets, forming a delightful shade, and sluices of water running at their feet.

APRIL 18TH. The city of Chihuahua (pronounced Che-wáh-wáh), the capital of the state of the same name, is well built, with wide clean streets, and handsome buildings; population from twelve to fifteen thousand. The plaza or public square, is large and imposing, adorned with a splendid fountain and seats, and pillars of white porphyry. On one side is a large and splendid cathedral, and the other sides are occupied by spacious public buildings, and stores. There are a large number of American merchants here. Dry goods are brought from the states, by the way of Sante-Fe. The trade to this place is large, and formerly was very profitable. There is a custom house here, notwithstanding many dry goods are smuggled in from the states. Provisions are very reasonable, and I am of opinion, it would make a pleasant place of residence. Water is brought from a distance by means of an aqueduct, and distributed through the town. According to the best authorities, Chihuahua is elevated above the sea 4638 feet, and some of the neighboring settlements, more than one mile.

REMARKS.

The articles of food most common in Mexico, and which soon become necessaries of life to a foreigner, are frejoles, chile, tortillas, penole, and atole. The frejole is a large brown bean, which is very rich, and everywhere used. It is generally boiled, and afterwards stewed in lard, and sometimes with a good sprinkling of chile. The chile, (red pepper), is liberally mixed with nearly all their dishes, meat and vegetable, and no true Mexican will pass the day without a dish of the genuine article itself. Even foreigners, who at first cannot endure its smart, soon become fond of its stimulant.

Tortillas are everywhere used, frequently with a rich gravy of chile, and with atole, a gruel made of penole. This they eat without knife or spoon; rolling the tortillas into a scoop, they dip up the liquid with admirable skill, and then devour the spoon itself.

The Mexicans are very punctual in the observance of the forms of religion, although they frequently go from the church to the gaming table, or cock fight, both priest and people.

The women, however, appear more devotional than the men. I have seen hundreds of females, early in the morning, kneeling in the great cathedral in this place, and perhaps one tenth as many men.

We have, more than once, been requested to doff our hats, when a priest passed in the street with the host, or on his way to visit the sick, and I have been told that in case of refusal to comply, that they would be forcibly taken off by the bystanders. As a matter of course, no intelligent foreigner will refuse to comply with the customs of a people, although they may not exactly accord with his notions of religious freedom.

All classes, both men and women, smoke cigarritos. A cigarrito is a small cigar, made of tobacco, rolled up in a white inodorous paper, or the thin inside husk of corn.

The men in traveling, carry a little bag of tobacco, paper cut of the right size, and a flint and steel. They often smoke the cigarrito as they ride along.

Copper coins are issued by the different states, and are not current out of the state in which they are coined. Small cakes of soap are a lawful tender in some of the states.

COINS.

1 onza	gold	16 dollars.
1 peso	silver	1 dollar.
1 real	silver	12 ½ cents.
1 medio	silver	6¼ cents.
1 quartillo	silver	3 ⅛ cents.
1 claco	copper	1 9/16 cents.

The Ranchero cultivates a farm, generally by peons, who he keeps in servitude. He delights in horses, is a fine rider, and fond of making excursions, attending fandangos, and is always ready to engage in wars, or guerilla expeditions. He is proud of fine trappings for his horse, wears a broad brimmed hat, with a large silver cord for a band; a fine serape or blanket, and generally carries his lasso in a coil on the pommel of his saddle. He is polite, a good companion, and passes the "buenas dias" with a good grace.

Peons are mostly the native Indians, who have been kept generally in a state of vassalage; although slavery is not recognized, their condition is not much better. Every facility is afforded them to sell themselves by getting in debt to the proprietors of the haciendas, and ranchos. By long oppression they have become servile, and in a measure contented with their condition, have become attached to the soil, and think, (knowing no other way of living), that the greatest evil that could befall them would be to be expelled from the land by the proprietors.

They are accustomed to submit to whippings like slaves, and their condition is probably in no respect better.

INDIANS.

The Apaches, and Camanches, two wandering tribes, are scattered over the extensive country, from Chihuahua to the river

Neuces [Nueces]. The Apaches are better warriors than the Camanches. They generally fight on fleet horses, which they manage
skillfully. They make their attacks by charging furiously into the
ranks of an enemy, shooting rapidly with their guns or bows, and
retreating as rapidly, before there is an opportunity to kill many of
them. They make excursions for robbing, every year, into several
states in Mexico, and always carry terror and desolation with them.
Since the fall of the Spanish power in Mexico, they have depopulated, and obtained possession of a large extent of country bordering on their own territory. They, every year, steal from the Mexicans, and drive into their own wild country, large numbers of
horses, mules, and cattle.[1]

There are but few wagon roads, and these are never repaired.
They are generally mere mule paths, cut by deep aroyos. Although
we passed over extensive plains and valleys, where the roads were,
from the nature of the ground, as good as a turnpike, yet we have
seen but one train of wagons from Brazos to this place. Goods are
carried on pack mules, and the Arrieros (muleteers) form a large
class in Mexico. They probably understand packing and managing
animals better than any other nation in the world. They carry a
cargo, about three hundred pounds on each animal, and the distance which they are allowed to travel per day, is regulated by law.
They camp whenever night overtakes them, or they find a suitable
place, and do not start in the morning until about 10 o'clock,
without stopping again, till they camp for the night. Travelers,
generally, are armed with pistols, and sometimes with swords and
muskets. The padres, (priests), and Alcaldes, who are the most
important personages in the towns, take great pride in keeping
fire-arms, and at several places where we stopped, they showed us
some expensive duelling pistols and rifles, and were anxious to
purchase our revolvers.

These gentlemen we invariably found polite and obliging, and
were the best authorities from whom we could obtain correct
information.

APRIL 19TH. Intending to make arrangements for our journey, I called a meeting of the company in the morning, to decide whether we should start in the afternoon, and for other business. Briggs was chosen 1st Lieutenant, and Searls 2nd. A committee of two was appointed to call upon the Miss. company, camped near us, to ascertain whether they would like to travel with us for mutual protection. Their answer was in the affirmative, and that they would be ready at 1 P.M. All were not ready until 3 o'clock; Captain Harding not being ready, Duncan remained to bear him company. The Miss. company started before us, I staid behind to bring up the rear. Our pack mule hindered us on the road, so that we were left behind the company. Towards night a storm was observed in the mountains a few miles ahead, and the thunder soon began to roll over our heads. The main body hastened on to Sacramento, a rancho twenty-one miles from Chihuahua. At sundown it commenced to rain violently, and we soon became pretty well drenched. We proceeded on in the darkness, till about 8 o'clock, and finding it difficult to keep the road, stopped where we found some shrubs to which we might fasten our animals, and camped down in our wet clothes. There were Barker, Briggs, Burke, Morris, and myself. I slept soundly, and had some pleasant dreams of the neighborhood where I spent my childhood.

APRIL 20TH. This morning our little party left camp early, and went two miles to Sacramento, where the celebrated battle was fought under Colonel Doniphan, in the late war,[2] where we found the advance of our company, who had been here during the night. We obtained some milk for breakfast, and went on two miles farther, where we found some good grass and water, for the pack mules. We then went on to Sonce, a rancho situated on a rise of ground in a prairie of great extent, and of excellent grass, upon which were flocks of sheep, and herds of cattle. The shepherds follow the sheep on horseback, accompanied by dogs. We computed that we saw from one point on the road five thousand sheep, scattered in every direction over the extensive prairie. After obtaining provision, we went two leagues and camped by a little pond hole in the prairie, where there was no wood. We attempted to cook some beef with grass, turf, and dried horse chips.

APRIL 21ST. We started at sunrise, intending to overtake the Miss. company, which had gone on, the night before, to a rancho, three leagues. Arnold and two others started ahead, intending to walk awhile and lead their animals. When he had gone a short distance he missed his spur, and gave his larriate to a comrade, to lead his mule. His rifle was slung on his saddle, which caused it to turn, upon which the mule commenced stamping, broke his saddle, tore his water bag, broke his rifle stock off at the trigger, and otherwise injured his baggage. We stopped in the afternoon at a rancho, where some troops were stationed, with sentinels on the walls looking out for Indians, and camped a mile beyond, at a deserted rancho, where there was an excellent spring of water. It was the largest and best that we had seen in Mexico. The Miss. company camped with us. This is said to be a favorite camping place of the Apaches when they visit this section.

APRIL 22D. We left our camp at the deserted rancho, at sunrise, in company with the Miss. and Morris company. We traveled rapidly ten or twelve leagues, without finding water, but at that distance came to a place where it could be found by digging through the turf, and camped. There was no wood, and some of the company went a mile for a few shrubs. The Miss. company having nothing to eat kept on. The water stood near the surface of the ground, and formed a damp bed. The atmosphere was also very chilly, this being high ground. For two weeks past I have been afflicted at nights with rheumatic pains in the chest, and between the shoulders. The pain was so severe last night, that I got but little sleep after twelve o'clock. It is probably occasioned by sleeping on the ground at several places where it was damp.

APRIL 23D. The country we passed to-day, was in gentle slopes, covered with dry grass. We passed a low gap in a mountain, and descended into a wide valley. We then ascended a grade of about eight miles, at an angle of two or three degrees. Before arriving at

Carmen, in the afternoon, we saw at the top of a hill, at a distance, a horseman apparently observing us; and on going a little farther, we discovered a party with horses. On arriving at Carmen, a mile distant, we learned that they were Apaches. The men of the town were on the tops of their houses, looking with anxiety at the movements of the Indians. There was also a party on an old tower, upon the top of a hill, one fourth of a mile distant. The miserable village looked as though it might be taken by a dozen men. The Indians are in the habit of entering these places, and robbing them of what little they can find, and after abusing the miserable, cowardly people, and perhaps driving off a few mules and horses, which are the principal objects of these expeditions, they leave, to plunder some distant village or rancho, and then seek their wild country with their booty. The horses and mules they value, not only as beasts of burden, and as articles of trade, but they live upon their flesh. In the course of an hour some of the Miss. company, with Morris and his interpreter Robert, went out to visit the Indians. Morris carried a white flag. The chief, who was stationed at the top of a hill, advanced a little, but appeared to mistrust danger. The Americans continued advancing, cautiously, and the chief kept men running over the hill to communicate with the main body. Morris requested the chief to order his men to halt, and the chief wished him to do the same. They accordingly did so,— and the chief wished to know who those men were, and what they wanted. He was told that they were friends. Morris then tried through his interpreter to signify that they wanted horses, and mules, and wished to trade; but the chief suspecting danger retired. They care but little for goods, their principal object being animals, and they are very loath to loose [lose] any of their warriors. The fact was, certain of the southerners, as I understood, were anxious to procure a few scalps, as there was a bounty paid for them by government. They were armed with rifles, muskets, lances, bows and arrows.[3] We had a beef killed at this place. Some of it we jerked, by cutting it in long thin strips and drying it over a slow fire.

APRIL 24TH. Our road passes over wide plains and gentle slopes, with occasionally a low smooth mountain at our right and left, entirely covered with grass. We occasionally see a herd of deer, but they are very shy. Camped at a small brook at dark, where there was once a rancho. We have traveled rapidly twelve leagues, without water.

APRIL 25TH. I suffered much the past night from pains in my knees, which are badly swollen. I think it has been occasioned partly by riding all day of late. It coming my turn to stand on guard, I would not refuse, as some of the company complain a little.

We arrived at Galeana at half past ten. Distance from Carmen fifteen leagues, without a rancho. This village contains perhaps two thousand inhabitants. In the afternoon we traveled five leagues, and camped upon the side of a mountain, where we found some water, which was apparently the section of a small brook, that ran out of the ground for a short distance and disappeared.

APRIL 26TH. Last night was kept awake several hours by pains in my knee, which is so bad that I am not able to bear my weight on it without excruciating pain. We passed in the morning what appeared to be a copper mine in the side of the mountain, as verdigris appeared running down the side. At noon we came to a river, where there was a grove of cottonwoods, and fine grass. In the afternoon we camped on the river bank. Not being able to obtain sleep on account of the increasing pain in my limb, I got up and sat against a tree, during the night. About midnight we heard the report of six guns in the road, half a mile ahead. Two of the Miss. company went to ascertain the cause, but could find none. In the morning we passed some Mexicans, camped by the river, loaded with wood. They said they had been firing to keep off the wolves.

APRIL 27TH. We passed through the silver mines at Baranco [Barranca], early.[4] The ore contains lead, copper, silver, and some gold. Five miles beyond is Coriolitas [Corralitos], a considerable village, at which place there are also furnaces for silver ore. All the neighboring mountains are said to be rich in metals. We camped by the side of the river, one half mile from Coriolitas, and the company spent the day in getting their animals shod, purchasing a stock of bread for the wilderness, &c. They had baked for them a kind of hard bread, which was very good.

I experienced great pain from my knee during the day, and was not able to leave camp. A mustard poultice was applied at night, but I was obliged to sit up the greater part of it, and got but little sleep.

APRIL 28TH. I managed to get upon my mule, when we started in the morning, with some assistance. Morris' man Bob, it was discovered had left in the night, and taken his best mules and two pistols with him. The weather was very warm, and I suffered intensely on the road. When we stopped at noon to graze, where there were some small shrubs, I was lifted from my mule, and lay upon the ground, with a blanket thrown over me, in great pain, not being able to obtain a shade. In the afternoon we reached Janos, eight leagues. I took Sam and went immediately in search of a room, and finally rode to the Alcalde's and lay in the court, until he came home, in about two hours. Briggs then came from the camp, and with one arm around his neck, and the other around that of the Alcalde, I managed to swing to a room, which was a large common one, and used as a sleeping apartment by several members of the family. Briggs then returned to camp, with the understanding that some one should come and stay with me. I had hoped to find a bed of some sort, and had on that account refused several rooms in town, that were not thus furnished. Some dried hides were thrown upon the ground, and my blankets laid on them. There are no floors to the best of their houses. I was obliged to lie in certain positions, from the fact that the cords of my legs had drawn and made them crooked, so that it was painful to lie on such a hard surface. After lying down, the Alcalde's mother assisted to take off my clothes. It was sometime before she could understand what was the matter with my knee. After examining it, she pronounced it the "reumatismo doloroso." She said that she once had it for two years, and suffered a great deal from it. She showed me every kindness and attention. I could get but little sleep. One end of the room, (which was very long), was occupied by the old lady and some children. Just before night, I learned that a train of seven hundred pack mules passed Sonora, on their way to Chihuahua, laden with produce and provisions. The companies untied and purchased a large beef of them for fifteen dollars, most of which they jerked for the journey.

We here received information that a party of five, or seven Americans and two Mexicans, were lately attacked on the Santa Fe road. Both the Mexicans, and all the Americans but two were killed. One of them who was wounded, made his escape to a rancho thirty miles distant.

APRIL 29TH. Mr. Barker came to see me in the morning, and remained about two hours. During the day I was visited by Dr. Adams and Copp of the Miss. company, their interpreter Mr. Kiggler and some members of our company. At night I took a few drops of laudanum, in consequence of which I obtained a few hours sleep.

RECUPERATION IN JANOS

April 30 – May 12, 1849

AT 9 O'CLOCK Dr. Adams and Copp with six or eight of our
company came to bid me farewell. Janos is the last place for a great
distance, and bordering on the Apache country, is looked upon as a
frontier town, on this route.[1] There is no person in the place who
can speak English. I was laid on my back and could with difficulty
be moved. I had shared with the company in their hardships and
dangers for three months, and now I was to be parted from them,
and left alone perhaps fifteen hundred miles from the place of our
destination, and how long, was more than any one could tell.

Shortly after they had all left me, being left alone, I fell into a
very sound and singularly oppressive sleep. When I awoke, I found
that my lame foot had got off the clothing, and lay upon the
ground, and that I had in consequence taken cold in it, which
made it somewhat worse. The old lady tries to stuff me with meat,
and hearty food. I tell her that too much meat is not good for my
lame knee, she is not satisfied, but says, putting her hand on my
breast, that it is good for one who has a sick heart. In the afternoon
about half a dozen ladies came to see me, and sat for an hour. The
old lady, I discovered, had a great deal to tell them about me; how I
was getting very poor, and would not eat, &c. They possess great
skill in keeping up the interest of conversation; one is ready to
begin just as another finishes, and all speaking with the greatest
distinctness, and volubility. At dusk two or three joined in singing
some songs in the court, which seemed to me as sweet as any thing
I ever heard. They excel greatly on the high notes, which they
strike with perfect ease. Their songs contain some fine variations,
and are very pretty. The Alcalde has had several talks with me, and
tells me not to be "triste," (sad).

MAY 1ST. The Alcalde tells me that he became acquainted with

Colonel Graham, who spent several days with him when passing here. Also with Colonel Cooke, and McClown. He said, using the little English he knew, "McClown my friend," and "buenos" man. He then said, addressing me, that "he was my friend;" I gave him my hand. He asked me in the presence of some ladies whether I was "contentas," [happy] or whether I was "triste." He then told them how I was affected when the Americans left. I told him I was not much sad, but after they had tried to inform me that they would do all they could for me, and that I must try to feel contented, I told them that I was not "triste" with a good Alcalde, and good senoras. We have some amusing times in finding the meaning of words, and sometimes spend considerable time by way of illustration, before finding them out, but we seldom give it up.

MAY 2D. I have used various methods with my knee, but nothing does it any good. Red pepper poultice relieved it for a short time, as also cold water applications, but its violence soon returns. A Mexican this afternoon recommended leeches, and the Alcalde promises to try to obtain some tomorrow. He informs me that a large company of Americans have arrived at Coriolitas, and will be here tomorrow. Oh, that I were able to go with them.

At the pealing of the bells, at dusk, some of the family always engage in evening worship, repeating their prayers. I have heard the wife of the Alcalde repeating, while her two little boys were obliged to give the response, or repeat a certain part in concert, which they did in a very rapid, and accurate manner, until the little fellows becoming sleepy, and tired out, cried from weariness; but were obliged to keep on, though in a pitiful tone. I have no doubt but the woman thinks she is doing her duty faithfully by her children. She is very beautiful and accomplished for a Mexican lady, and her children pretty. There are besides these boys, one girl of six years, and one younger. Nearly every night the little girl comes timidly into my room, kneels facing me, and repeats a prayer; I conclude that it is intended for my benefit, and that she is directed to do so. It is at any rate affecting for me to see her. I have been more comfortable, and slept nearly half the night.

MAY 3D. The Alcalde obtained four little leeches, but they would not take hold. I am getting impatient, that I am getting no better, for fear that all the companies for this year, will be past, before I am able to go. The doctors told me on leaving, that I might be ready to leave in a few weeks, and it might be six months. The rainy season commences here in about a month.

MAY 4TH. An American called on me this morning, who belongs to a company, who are coming from Coriolitas in the afternoon. The company arrived before night. It is made up of Jordan's and others, and numbers only eighteen. Morris came from Coriolitas with them. There is a company with a number of wagons expected from Chihuahua. If no other opportunity offers, I hope to be able to go along with them. I slept none at night, to do me any good.

MAY 5TH. Morris and Burke called to see me. They have concluded to wait till the company arrives with wagons. They are encamped about three miles out. A company of Apaches, a part of them women, arrived at the Alcalde's in the afternoon. They were very noisy, particularly the women, whose actions and appearance are more disgusting than any people that I ever saw. They seemed delighted in talking very loud, and in uttering uncouth and apparently unmeaning sounds, at which the others would laugh loud and long. Some of the women stayed all night, and slept in the room with the old lady.

MAY 6TH. The Alcalde left to-day for Coriolitas, with his wife and sister, who are going to make a visit there of several days. His mother, for some cause which I could not understand, was much opposed to it, and affected by it, and came and told me about it in a long discourse, which, of course I could not fully understand. She even shed tears in trying to persuade her son to remain at home. He appeared to feel unpleasantly about it, and paced the room back and forth, in a most thoughtful manner. When they left, his wife and sister came to bid me farewell. I did not see them again, as they had not returned when I left.

MAY 8TH. The old lady has several times ground some herbs, in which she has great faith, upon a stone, in my presence, and rubbed it upon my knee. I perceived a very unpleasant smarting sensation from it, but no beneficial effects.

MAY 9TH. I am using aguardiente and red pepper, hot, upon my knee. It reduces the swelling a little, but nothing avails to relax the cords, so that I can bend it at all. The fluid from the joint has formed a sack, holding perhaps half a tea-cup full. The left knee is also affected, in a less degree. My eyes, which on my arrival, were more inflamed than ever before in my lifetime, and had been quite troublesome on the road, are getting much better. The old lady applied a kind of gum, which she called mesquite, and which proved an effectual remedy. For the last two or three days, before arriving here, they were so inflamed, that I was obliged to keep them shut the greater part of the time, when riding on the sandy road, in the hot sun.

Not having been able to obtain any refreshing sleep, when I have greatly needed it, I have been troubled, several nights, with some of the strangest vagaries and fancies, even while I thought, and should ordinarily call myself awake.

I one night fancied,—but it appeared more like a reality than a dream, and I seemed more awake than asleep,—I fancied that I was camped a little out of town, upon the ground as usual. It seemed as though each limb of my body, was a person, for whom I had to care and provide, and that they had all got out of bed, and were groping about in the dark, among the hobbles of the cold ground, in great pain and distress, and they were not able to find the bed, where we had camped. After apparently spending several hours, thus unpleasantly employed, I accidentally laid my hand on the bed, and immediately found the side of the room, when I became conscious of my true situation. I had rolled out of my apology for a bed, composed of ox hides and sheep skins, and had been strolling about the room, without being able to find it again, until I had become chilled, and my limbs pained me.

Another night I awoke, and found myself taking off my shirt. I immediately saw what I was about, and its impropriety, yet, as if moved by some impulse, previously received, which I could not resist, I kept on, and took it off. In the morning I found it by my side. The adobe houses with dirt floors, are damp and chilly, but as the blankets fortunately kept on, I did not take cold.

The women here, who occasionally call, seem if possible to inherit a greater propensity, and possess a greater faculty for talking, than with us. I have known one to talk incessantly for half an hour, so as not to allow another to edge in a monosyllable, except it might be one of affirmation or negation, which is of course always allowable. This they frequently accompany with expressive gestures, and great modulations of voice.

I think the Spanish language more musical, and better adapted to conversation than ours. The old lady is still greatly concerned lest I shall starve, and brings in her dishes, hot, with their favorite chile, and complains if I refuse them. Burke spent several hours with me to-day.

MAY 10TH. About sundown, a large number of Apaches, men and women, came into the court, on one side of which my room is situated. I had heard them yelling in the streets, for sometime, but thought it was boys playing. They kept up a constant hubbub until nine o'clock. Occasionally one of the women would raise her voice in a most shocking *"catawaul,"* when the rest would join in a loud laugh. Most of them left at nine o'clock, but in about an hour, a loud knocking was heard at the door of the outside wall. It was not heeded for sometime, but at length one of the peons was sent to the door, when they went off. In a hour there was another lumbering and screaming at the door. I hear them in the street nearly all night. The Alcalde of this place and the Apaches are now on terms of peace; this state of things has recently been brought about.[2] They visit the town every few days to trade; they sell mules and horses which they had stolen, dried beef, &c., and get in exchange, aguardiente, clothing, and a few other things. They soon become intoxicated with aguardiente, and commence their noise, and the

Alcalde seems to suffer it as a necessary evil. The Alcalde sold two mules to one of the companies, which he has purchased from them, [the Apaches] and which had on them the government brand. It was thought that they were stolen from El Passo. The authorities either are obliged, or find it for their interest, to wink at these things. This being a frontier town, bordering on the Indian territory, the inhabitants have generally been obliged to keep close at home for fear of the Indians.

An old man, the other day, told me that he had never been over the mountain, in sight of this place; he had known several who had gone over and never returned. Under such slavish fear are they of the Indians. They always carry their arms with them, when they go out of town with their animals to graze, or for other purposes.

A certain gentleman, who has often traveled in the wake of our company, and is now camped two or three miles out, was the other day walking very leisurely from town to camp, without any arms, when he was met by three Apaches, mounted, who surrounded him with their lances aimed at his breast, while all that he could do in the confusion of the moment, was to pretend to be feeling in his bosom for a pistol. He finally had presence of mind enough to stammer out "amigo," (friend,) when they let him pass, saying that they wished to know whether he was friend or foe; it broke him however of his habit of strolling about unarmed.

MAY 12TH. This morning, with the aid of a chair for support, I made my way to the door, which is the first time I have looked out for fourteen days. I cannot yet bear my weight on my right leg. The wagons from Chihuahua are expected every day, and it seems like my last hope, to get into one of them, as there is no probability that I can ride my mule at present. Morris called yesterday afternoon, and as he had traded a horse for provisions, he promised to furnish me with hard bread, dried meat, &c., and send it before night. Some Apaches came in the afternoon; one man, who was remarkably loquacious, came up and shook hands; he then laid one hand on my breast, and asked, "Este bueno?" (is it good, or well.) I answered, "bueno." He then placed his hand on his heart, and said, "Este bueno." Although he professed that his heart was well disposed toward me, yet from his savage and repulsive appearance, I would not like to trust him.

Before night some members of the company from Chihuahua came in and informed me that the wagons and about seventy men had arrived, and would leave by sunrise in the morning. My anxiety to go with them was very great. I knew not what to do; I could not walk, and was left in a state of suspense until near sundown, when Burke came in bringing with him Dr. Scott, from Mississippi, with whom I first became acquainted at Camargo. Very seldom in my lifetime have I been more rejoiced to see any one, as I knew his kind disposition, and felt that something would now be done.

He had heard of my situation on his arrival, and expressed surprise at seeing me here, supposing that by this time I was on the Gila. He informed me that Gov. McNees,³ the director of the train, had promised to take me into one of his wagons, in consideration of my helpless condition, although he had repeatedly refused to take a pound more of loading. Mr. McNees is from Missouri, but has for sometime been trading to Chihuahua. He was in California last year, and left about the time that there first began to be talk of gold. He has five wagons, with four pairs of mules each, besides a large number of loose mules. He had agreed to carry the baggage of a large number of men, at Chihuahua, in consideration of which, they were to pay a certain sum, and act as guards to the train.

I immediately got my little baggage together and took leave of the family. The Alcalde would accept of no compensation, saying that mine was a "mala fortuna," (bad fortune.) I however made him the small present of a fine shirt, a box of caps, and a purse. For the old lady, I could think of nothing in my possession but a teaspoon. With the aid of my friends, I got upon my mule and rode down to camp, and once more slept in the open air. I rested better than for sometime before.

THROUGH GUADALUPE PASS TO SANTE CRUZ ON GRAHAM'S ROUTE

May 13–25, 1849

MAY 13TH. Soon after sunrise, with a little assistance, I managed to get into one of the wagons, which is of the regular Sante Fe order, with a cover, and fixed myself the best I could on some sacks of corn, with my blankets about me. We soon after started on our journey. Morris had not furnished me with the provisions which I engaged of him, which left me with a very short allowance. From this place there is nothing but a trail. We take Graham's route.[1] He passed here last fall, with about a hundred wagons, some say more, some less, and a large number of mules. To pass over such mountains, and through such a wilderness, with wagons, is a great undertaking. The road this morning lay over a plain, thickly sprinkled with loose stones, and with an occasional gulley. We camped after noon, in a little valley, where several small ponds were connected by a small stream; quite a romantic spot. In the morning, Morris with several companies, numbering about seventy, passed us. Our number was nearly the same. I asked Morris if he would let me have the provisions which I engaged; he replied that we should overtake him, and then I should have them. Sometime before he had borrowed my note books; I had several times asked him for them, and he had as often promised to send, or bring them to me. He now told me they were in his baggage, and he would give them to me when he stopped. It put me to much inconvenience. He wished to borrow them to ascertain the distances, &c. I was however informed that he had been very busy in drawing them off; that some publishers in New York had offered a certain sum for a journal of the route, and he was now trying to make it out. When we arrived at the water, the companies had all left, and Morris with them. They had watered their animals, and probably went on ten or fifteen miles farther without water.

MAY 14TH. We continued crossing the stony plain with mountains on our left, along the sides of which are stunted oaks. The governor's men consist of Mexicans, French, Irish, Negroes, Americans and Scotch. We have nearly all the lingo of Babel, a motley crew, but good-natured and sociable. Some of the men have lived in New Mexico and the territories, and others are the hardy fur-hunters. One little Frenchman who has been living in Central Mexico, can speak several languages, but has them all mixed up, and probably speaks his native tongue as badly as any. It is sometimes amusing to hear him, as he will often commence conversing in one language, and forgetting himself go off on another, and end with the third. Distance 10 leagues.

MAY 15TH. We approached the mountains; at their foot we passed through a grove of oaks, a mile in width, which in appearance very much resemble an old apple orchard, the lower limbs being dead. The trail over the mountains is very faint, as there probably has never been but two trains of wagons across them. It winds along the mountain sides, and over some very steep places. For my own part, while living quietly in New England, I never once dreamed that an eight mule team, with a large wagon, could be got over such mountains, and across such difficult ravines. I do not believe that Hannibal carried his baggage into Italy by a more difficult mountain passage. We passed over some ravines, the sides of which seemed pretty closely approaching the perpendicular. At some places we were surrounded on all sides by mountains, where at first view there seemed no possible way of escape. Having ascended a long and difficult grade we reached the summit. From this point I beheld as I sat perched in the wagon, probably one of the finest views in nature. We looked down upon an extensive valley, luxuriant with grass, and studded with hillocks, with mountains of different heights at its circumference. At our feet lay a beautiful little lake, sparkling in the sun. We descended the long and steep declivity with all the wheels locked, slowly and cautiously, arrived safely in the valley, and camped among the fine grass, near a spring of cold water; I hobbled to the branch that ran from it, and bathed in its gelid stream. Bathing in cold water is recommended for the rheumatism by those who have lived in this climate.

Just at night one of the men brought in a fine deer, which was liberally distributed. As it is considered a dangerous place for the Indians to stampede the mules, among these mountains, they put eight men on guard at a time. The governor's mules go together, and are tended by Mexicans. They are kept out to grass till ten o'clock at night, when they are brought into a corral, formed by placing the wagons in a circle, and stretching ropes from one to the other; they are then fed with corn, and driven to grass again before light.

MAY 16TH. Still among the mountains. If I were to use my Yankee privilege, I should "guess" that we were obliged to lock our wheels a hundred times during the day. At one hill, they were obliged to put twelve mules to each wagon, and as many men as were able to get about it to push. It was with great difficulty that they were drawn up, although they did not contain as much loading as is usually given to two animals. We camped in a little valley, by the bed of a small steam, where the water was standing in pools. A vigilant guard is kept up, for fear of the Indians driving off the mules. My lameness recovers but slowly. One of our hunters brought in an antelope. On the steep sides of the mountains I observed many stunted cedars.

MAY 17TH. We commenced the passage of the Gaudalupe pass [Guadalupe Pass].[2] This is supposed to be the only one for several hundred miles north or south, which can be made by wagons, and with but few exceptions, with pack mules, from the great table lands of Mexico. It is a ravine with precipitous mountains rising on each side, through which flows a rivulet. In the narrow valley are some sycamore trees. We stopped at ten on a small flat where there was grass, to refresh our animals. I noticed a solitary butternut tree, the only one I have seen in the country. Birds were singing among the trees, in the gorge of the mountain. We have seldom heard their music of late. One of the men brought in a squirrel; this is the first that I had seen, although gophers and armadillos are plenty. I took this opportunity to bathe in the creek. My ride in the wagon, over such a road as this, cannot with propriety be called a ride for pleasure. We left at two o'clock. The trail (for it is nothing more) ran along the creek, and part of the way in its channel, very rough with stones and many gulleys. Part of the time, I lie stretched upon what blankets I can find, at other times I sit up and hold upon the sides of the wagon. During the stoppages, which are frequent, I am improving the time in reading a book entitled "What I Saw in California," by Bryant, lent me by Dr. Scott.³ Camped near the creek with grass, I am able to walk around the camp a little.

MAY 18TH. Leaving camp at 7 o'clock, we worked our way along the creek by a very rough passage, sometimes being obliged to cut down trees. After proceeding slowly for an hour, a man rode up from the rear, and informed the Governor that the tongue had broken from one of the wagons. We had nothing more to do but stop, turn out our teams to grass, and wait for the wagon to be mended. About 4 o'clock, the tongue being replaced, we went a mile farther and camped. Distance one league.

MAY 19TH. We left the bed of the creek, and climbed the side of the mountain by regular ascent, so that the road was not difficult. Having reached the top of the grade, the trail for several miles ran over an elevated, stony plain. Before us lay an extensive valley of fertile land. At 4 o'clock we reached the bottom of this beautiful valley, where is a large tract of low land, forming excellent pasturage. On a bluff at the edge of the bottom, is an old deserted rancho, which has the appearance of having once been extensive. We camped at this place, there being no water for twenty-five or thirty miles ahead. In the afternoon we had a strong wind from the south-west.⁴

MAY 20TH. Starting at sunrise we passed the extensive ruins of the rancho Santa Bernardino, the walls of which are fortified with regular bastions. They are situated on a rise of ground, with a beautiful grassy flat on each side, with a small creek running through it, upon one of which we camped last night, and beyond which is a bluff from ten to thirty feet high, which forms the level of an extensive plain; beyond these, mountains can be seen rising in the distance. It is one of the prettiest valleys I have ever seen. It has been depopulated by the Indians. They have been getting the upper hand of the Mexicans since the fall of the Spanish power, as the numerous deserted ranchos and towns through this whole region testify. Upon the table land, is a shrub, two or three feet high, called grease wood, from the fact that it burns like grease when put upon the fire. Passing over a mountain, at a place where the passage was not difficult, we came in view of another valley fifteen or eighteen miles across. Having reached the bottom of the valley at twelve o'clock, we stopped to graze our animals, and take our dinner. We then traveled till sundown, and camped without water. Distance, ten or eleven leagues.

MAY 21ST. Starting early, we traveled about a league, when coming to water, we stopped. There are many herds of wild cattle in these valleys; they are much more wild and dangerous than buffaloes.[5] They were introduced here by the Indians, who stole them from the Mexicans, in the depredations on their settlements, and probably some of them are from the stock that formerly belonged to the old rancho Sante Bernardino. Yesterday our company killed two of them.

An adventure with these cattle, was related by a member of the N. Adams Company that we afterward overtook. He left the company with a gentleman from Mississippi, and rode among a range of small hills, off from the road, in search of beef. They soon discovered an old bull, grazing over a knoll. After fastening their mules, they fired at him several times without his taking much notice of them; finally the Mississippian ventured a little nearer and discharged his gun, when the enraged animal rushed down the hill, and taking him on his horn, tossed him into the air. His friend coming up at that instant, fired, and fortunately killed him. The Mississippian escaped with slight injury.

It is surprising to see with what admirable precision the teamsters, who are Sante Fe men, drive their mule teams, in the most difficult places. The trail runs over mountains, and through ravines, where it would seem impossible for a wagon to pass. When a mule disobeys, he generally gets a suitable whipping. The drivers talk a great deal to their teams, as though they were intelligent.

When we make a stop of several hours, some of the men who are blacksmiths, are employed in shoeing the mules. They have brought along the shoes and nails, ready made, and have the tools necessary for putting them on. In the afternoon, we went a short distance and camped. The road lay over an undulating country. Distance, four leagues.

MAY 22D. The road lay through a fine grass country, and good traveling. Coming to water a little before sundown, we camped by it. Since leaving Sante Bernardino, there has been a plenty of grass, and the land gently undulating. Laing, who is a celebrated western hunter, killed a beef.

MAY 23D. We traveled until near sundown, when coming to a rough mountain pass, Kniel, who professed to act as our guide, having been through the route with Graham's troops, suddenly came to the conclusion that we were on the wrong trail. So turning back, at dark we found another trail, leading out of the one in which we had been traveling, taking which, we soon came to water and camped for the night. We saw an Antelope this afternoon.

MAY 24TH. After traveling an hour, the trail took a turn, when Kniel became sure we were right, which was gratifying to us all, as its direction when we left the other trail was north-east, but it afterward turned more to the north, and then to the north-west. Several men last night were out hunting cattle, and not finding our camp in season, they camped by themselves. When they left their camp in the morning, Mr. Rice from Charlemont, Mass., was sitting by the fire; some of the company asked him if he was not coming on. He told them to go on and he would overtake them. Not arriving in our camp, some men fearing that the Indians had found him, went to search, but were not able to find him. There was considerable anxiety among us during the day concerning him. After arriving at our camp at night, rather unexpectedly to us, he came in. His mule had got away from him, and took a straight course across the mountains to Sante Cruz, and he followed after him.[6] A little before night we arrived upon a bluff at the end of a fine valley or basin, with Sante Cruz in view, about three miles distant. Entering this valley we camped on a small stream. Distance eight leagues.

MAY 25TH. Early in the morning, we passed through Sante Cruz, and camped half a mile on the other side. We spent the day in procuring provisions. On going into the town, we met the men going into the fields to work, all armed with guns and spears. I took notice of an answer given by my driver, a Sante Fe man. Asking him what they did with their guns and lances, he said, "When they see the Indians coming, they throw them down and run like h———l."

Sante Cruz is a small, compactly built place; some parts of it in ruins. On each side of the town there is a beautiful fertile valley. There is a flouring mill, which was erected by a Yankee who afterward went to California. Unbolted wheat flour was to be had, but scarce; it costs from 75 to 87½ cents per almuer, about six quarts. Penole, made of wheat, was plenty; I saw them making it where I purchased mine. The wheat is soaked in hot water, then put into frames to drain, from which it is taken and spread on hides to dry in the sun; it is then put into a large oven and parched or baked, when it is ready to grind. The flouring is generally done by mules or asses, in this part of Mexico. Penole makes an excellent food for the journey, made into a pudding, or porridge; sweetened and stirred in water, it makes a very refreshing drink. As no dried meat was to be found, I procured some fresh, which I jerked on the road, when we stopped. We visited many houses in this place; it is customary to enter without ceremony. I spent several hours at the place where my bread was baking, and had another opportunity to observe the manners of the people. In many of their habits the Mexicans are very filthy. I more than once saw a woman wash her hands in a drinking gourd, which was kept on the top of the water jar, and used every few minutes by some one for drinking. The following is an instance of the strength of the Indians, (Apaches,) and their command over the Mexican inhabitants on their borders. During planting time, this year, while the men of this village were at work in the field, a party of Indians presented themselves, and demanded a fine horse, the best in town. If it was not delivered to them, they declared that they would not allow a blade of corn to grow in the valley this season. The owner immediately gave him up without resistance. The women are very anxious to procure jewelry, handkerchiefs, &c.

TO THE PRESIDIO OF TEUSON AND ACROSS A DESERT TO THE GILA RIVER

May 26 – June 3, 1849

MAY 26TH. I had so far recovered from my lameness that I determined to try to ride my mule to-day. Governor McNees has carried me in his wagon from Janos, two hundred miles, which has taken twelve days. With disinterested generosity, he would accept of no compensation, neither would he receive any for carrying my provisions still farther on the road. As we have now come again into what has been a settled country, we again find, what has been, a kind of road. It passes down the valley of the Rio San-Pedro. [1] The river is bordered with cottonwoods. The valley is from one to four miles wide. The mountains bordering the valley are covered with stunted oaks; this valley would make a delightful abode for civilized man. Dr. Scott has taken my place in the wagon, with rheumatism, being in great pain, and not able to move. Two deer were killed to-day. Distance six or seven leagues.

MAY 27TH. Three of the men attacked a grizzly bear last night on the other side of the river. They felled him three times, but their ammunition gave out. He was running towards one of the men, whose gun was yet loaded with buck shot, when coming very near, he let it blaze into his face, when they all ran, the men in one direction and the bear in another; this was the last that they saw of him. In the morning, they went out again, and tracked him by his blood some distance. After having traveled two or three miles, this morning, I discovered that I had left my belt and pistols at the camp. I rode back after them alone, as fast as I could urge my mule, although it was not very pleasant, as we saw signs of Indians near, and a corral they had used, and they are in the habit of lurking about camps. I found the grass about the camp on fire, and spreading rapidly. The road is pretty good down this splendid valley, although in some places rather rough, from thick tufts of grass, that have grown up in it since it has been used. Trees are becoming common on the river; its direction is indicated by them for a long distance. They are principally cottonwoods, with some sycamore, willow, and mesquite. A fawn was brought into camp in the evening. Distance nine leagues.

MAY 28TH. At noon, we passed a castle situated under the mountain, whose walls presented a fine appearance. The large church had a dome resembling the State house, in Boston. The castle was deserted not long since. As we were passing by, half a mile distant, some of the company who had gone to visit it, commenced ringing the bell, which brought to mind the joyful sound of the church bell at home, and of civilization, in this solitary place. The church connected with the castle, was said by those who visited it, to be very splendid, with gilding, &c., and in good repair. Peaches, pears and quinces, were found growing in the garden. In the mountains, at the base of which stands the castle, is a rich gold mine. It had not long been discovered, and a company of Mexicans were obtaining large quantities of gold, without the aid of proper tools, using their ramrods, &c., when they were driven away by the Apaches, last February. A few miles below, we passed through San Pedro, a town from appearance, deserted within a year past. The inhabitants were driven off in such haste as not to be able to carry many of their cooking utensils, baskets, bowls, jars, &c., such as are in use with them. Some of our men took some earthen pots to cook in. The two bells were hanging in the tower of the church. Before I had arrived, one of the men had unfastened one of them, and tumbled it to the ground. It was a fine toned one. In one of the buildings was a mill for grinding. Fruit trees were growing in enclosures near the houses, and the whole looked more desolate than Goldsmith's "Deserted Village." Passing through the town we camped near the river, on some fine grass. Distance eight or nine leagues.

MAY 29TH. We passed a few miles farther along the Rio San Pedro, the road has been along its banks for three or four days, perhaps seventy-five miles. It passes through one of the most beautiful and fertile valleys in the world, once inhabited by the Mexicans, but now presenting a melancholy spectacle of deserted ranchos, and fields running to waste. We procured water, in places from zequias [*acequias*] which were used to irrigate the land. This valley is well adapted for grazing, and is capable of supporting large herds of cattle. The Indians, now, have undisputed possession. It must be a miserable race that could deliver up such a valley, with its delightful climate.

On leaving the river we entered upon a barren plain. We noticed at this point, human bones scattered about, and skulls stuck upon the bushes. This was probably once the battle ground of the Mexicans and Indians. In the afternoon, coming to some large cacti, we cut into them to procure water to quench our thirst. In this way the lives of famishing travelers are sometimes saved. The cactus fortunately grows in some of the most parched deserts. The kind that affords water grows but a little out of the ground, in the shape of a straw beehive, some as large around as a half bushel. Their taste is like a green watermelon. Coming into bottom land again, at sundown, we traveled until 8 o'clock, some men in the mean time riding out in search of water. Coming to a grassy meadow, where judging from the nature of the ground, as well as we could in the darkness, that there must be water not far off, we camped. Several men went out in different directions, and soon found a small creek with high banks. We had come twenty-five miles without water, and we considered ourselves fortunate in at last finding it, in the darkness. Distance 12 leagues.

MAY 30TH. In the morning we passed through San Gabriel, a village inhabited by Indians and Mexicans. There is a large church with two towers, which probably cost as much as all other buildings in the town. The place bears the appearance of once having been flourishing. The Indians are partly Pimos, and partly Apaches. Several hundred were camped on a creek near the town. Nine miles farther we came in sight of the Presidio of Teuson [Tucson], and finding good water and grass we camped. Learning that there is no water beyond two miles from Teuson, to the river Gila, about one hundred miles, the Governor determined to stop here, two or three days, to recruit the animals. Going to town, we were able to procure meats, bread, and flour. Milk was given to us in baskets, which are woven so closely, that they are used for containing liquids. The flour is ground in mills of the simplest construction. They consist of a bed stone about three feet in diameter, set on a mud platform with a channel surrounding it to catch the flour. The upper stone has a notch on each side, to which a level is tied with strings. It is turned by a mule or ass, attached to the lever.

There is a band of organized troops stationed here. The soldiers make a contemptible appearance, lounging about their quarters. Their pay is the promise of three bushels of wheat; and a small sum of money per month. The wheat they get, the money they do not. They however receive more than their services are worth. Distance ten miles.[2]

MAY 31ST. I obtained four mule shoes from the blacksmith, at one dollar apiece. The smith did not know how to put them on, although he was considered the best mechanic in town. I saw at this smith's shop, a natural curiosity. It was a piece of native iron from a neighboring mountain, used for an anvil, and the only one in the shop. It was between three and four feet long, with two large legs, which were firmly set in the ground, all in one piece, and judged by our men to weight two thousand pounds. I hammered it, and found it malleable.

JUNE 1ST. At eleven we moved to water on the other side of the town. Passing through, I purchased a basket of milk, holding more than two quarts, for six cents, a portion of which I put into my gourd to carry along. I had previously purchased a leather bag, holding about nine gallons, which I filled with water and put into a wagon, that I might have a little to spare for my mule, while crossing the desert. The wagoner was to have half for carrying it. At four in the afternoon we started from our second camp to make the great jornada, which we had been a long time dreading. We traveled until half past three next morning, over a dry road, and in places very sandy, a distance of thirty or forty miles.

JUNE 2D. Starting soon after sunrise, we traveled until 12 noon, when we stopped until 3 o'clock, where we found a little scattering grass. The country generally is a proper desert, and but little grass in any place. The weather seems warmer than any I ever before experienced, probably above 100° Fahrenheit, the greater part of the day. The animals suffered severely from thirst, and several horses "gave out," and were left behind. When an animal could proceed no farther, he was sometimes shot, at others he was left to his fate. The mules raised most piteous cries. When commenced by one, several would join in, as if from sympathy. My leather bag had leaked out about one half of the water. however I was able to give a little to my mule, which fared better than most of them. Towards night, it was difficult to hold some of the animals from rushing forward too fast. We overtook two men of a Mississippi company which left Teuson before us. We also passed two men on foot, who had been left behind by their company. They had become so much exhausted that they lay down at 12 o'clock at night upon the sand, without coats, or blankets. They were found the next day, nearly famished, by one who went back for a stray mule. I obtained a few minutes sleep two or three times in the night, by riding ahead of the teams, and lying down in the sand, after making the mule's lariate fast to my body, to prevent him from running away.

JUNE 3D. We arrived at the river Gila at 10 in the forenoon. The Mississippians say that they never saw as warm weather at home, as on this desert. There being no shade at our camp, we made one by throwing blankets over mesquite bushes, and clearing away the thorns for a lounge underneath. (By the way, we find thorns in Mexico on every bush.) We have managed thus through Mexico. The Gila (pronounced Hela) is rapid and narrow. On arriving at water the mules rushed forward, and it seemed difficult to allay their thirst. When the caballada [drove of horses] was driven down to the river, several of us were there watering our animals. When they had come over the high bank, in sight of the water, the Mexicans hallooed to us to take our mules away, or we should be

driven into the stream. All hastened away but a New York gentleman, who chose to take his own time, when the animals came
rushing on in a body. Some plunged into the water, and swam to a
bar in the middle of the river, and dragged our man into the
stream, to the great amusement of the rest. Three men fainted
yesterday upon the road. A Frenchman was brought in to-day, who
fell behind the company last night, and was found delirious and
nearly dead. He left his horse eight or ten miles back. A gentleman from New Orleans, formerly connected with the Picayune
[Durivage], "gave out" a few miles back, and lay under a bush,
while his negro man went on to water, and returned with some for
him. He had made up his mind to bleed a mule and drink the
blood, before the boy returned, but it was well he did not, as that
course generally proves fatal.[3] Those that were with the wagons
fared best, as they had water the whole way.

ALONG GEN. KEARNY'S AND MAJ. GRAHAM'S
ROUTES NEAR THE GILA RIVER TO THE JUNCTION OF
THE GILA WITH THE COLORADO RIVER

June 4–20, 1849

JUNE 4TH. We moved our camp about five miles down the river, to within four or five miles of the Pimos [Pimas'] village. Morris and the companies he was traveling with, left here the morning before we arrived. Many Pimos visited our camp, men and women, they brought for sale frijoles, or beans, flour, penole, salt, tortillas, and molasses, from the fruit of the pitahaya [pitaya cactus]. They would not take money for any thing near its value, but preferred beads, shirts, especially red flannel, pieces of old cloth, &c. The men wear but little clothing; a few had on old shirts that they had obtained from the Americans. The women, a cotton blanket, or piece of cotton cloth, which they manufacture, fastened around the waist. Their children they carry, fastened on frames upon their shoulders. They appear good-natured and sociable, and I have heard no complaint of their stealing. They do not speak the Spanish language, but there are a few individuals among them that have some knowledge of it. Their interpreter, who speaks Spanish, is an intelligent fine looking fellow. The name of the head chief is Juan Antonio.[1]

JUNE 5TH. A New York company arrived, and camped near us. We have an indolent time in camp, when compared with our tedious marches. While some lie in the shade of their booths and read, others walk around the camp and observe the Indians, who are plenty here at all times, with their baskets, and bundles of articles for sale, or visit the place of a neighbor, for each little mess of two or three, has cleared a path through the tall weeds to some mesquite bush, and formed a shade by hanging blankets around it. At night we take the blankets down to make our beds. The land on these bottoms is very fertile, soft, so that our feet sink into it, and of a dark color. The weeds are breast high, or more, and what grass there is to be found, is under the weeds. In places, however, there are good fields of grass free from weeds.

JUNE 6TH. This morning I made a washing day, having borrowed a camp kettle. I repaired to the river and made a fire under some cottonwoods in the bank, to heat the water.

JUNE 7TH. Leaving camp a little after sunrise, we passed down the river, and through the settlement of the Pimos. Their fields, which are formed by driving stakes into the ground, extend perhaps five miles down the river, and there are habitations scattered along the greater part of the way. Their wigwams are formed by driving poles into the ground, and bending them over, and fastening them at the top, in the shape of ovens. They are six or seven feet high, and from twenty to fifty feet in diameter, covered with wheat straw, and plastered with mud. They have also summer sheds, near some of their houses, which are simply platforms raised on stakes, and covered with mud, which are used as shades, and upon which they dry such provisions as need it. Being in want of a gourd, I went into several of their cabins before I was able to suit myself. They keep their molasses stowed away in jars, hermetically sealed. Their other provisions are also deposited in their cabins, principally in large baskets. I saw several carts made like those of the Mexicans. Their principal crop is wheat, which is now nearly ripe. I saw some watermelons growing. Corn was so little advanced that we were able to obtain but few roasting ears. They also raise beans, cotton, and pumpkins. Their agricultural implements consist of the axe, shovels, wooden hoes, and harrows. The soil is so easily pulverized that ploughs are not needed. Their domestic animals are chickens, dogs, horses, mules, and oxen.

The Pimos came out to the road to see us as we passed. Both they and the Coco Maricopas, who are associated with them, seem to be quiet people, living principally by agriculture, but although said to be naturally peaceable, they are considered good warriors when occasion requires. Their countenances are almost universally pleasing. They appear to be frank and simple, which is the reverse of the Apaches, their chief enemies, who are a wandering tribe, suspicious and treacherous, and get their living principally by stealing from the Mexicans. There seems to be, at the present time, a fine field for Missionary labor open among them. They would doubtless soon learn the arts and refinements of civilized life.

Nearly the whole of the Gila is drawn off by zequias for irrigating the land, which is laid out in little squares, with sluices between, to admit the water from the zequias. They obtain their salt from the low plains in the neighborhood, where it is found in the shape of efflorescence, after the rainy season. The Coco Maricopas live a few miles farther down the river; they are similar in dress and manners to the Pimos, but rather more athletic, and their countenances more intelligent. They speak a distinct language. Within a few years they have associated themselves with the Pimos, having come from about the mouth of the Gila. The two tribes number about two thousand.[2] This country will doubtless before long be settled by Americans.

Through the whole valley of the Gila are scattered ruins of very ancient adobe houses, some of them several hundred feet long, mounds of earth and brick; broken pottery, &c., the relics of the inhabitants of past ages. This country probably once supported a dense population. The present occupants have no certain knowledge of their more powerful predecessors, they have some very vague traditions and legends, in regard to them, which the more intelligent among them do not believe.[3]

An ancient dwelling of the ruins described is called a "Casa Montezuma."[4] They probably were built by the Aztecs. There is one nearly opposite the village, on the north side of the river, and they are numerous farther up the valley. Some of these have walls nearly perfect. Having traveled about sixteen miles, we camped on low ground, where we found some holes dug for water, which was impregnated with soda; and one of them contained sulphur. We found a Mississippi company encamped here. On our left is a bluff, with mountains in the rear. While on the other hand a vast plain of grass extends to a great distance. This is a fine place to recruit our animals. About half a mile on this plain we found some water.[5]

JUNE 8TH. At the Pimos village I associated myself as messmate with Dr. Joseph E. Field, of the North Adams, (Mass.) company. Messrs. Temple and Rice of the same company were also with the wagons. Dr. Field was surgeon in the Texan army, and was one of the two who were spared at the massacre of Colonel Fanning's [Fannin's] regiment. The doctor and myself went out in the morning and collected in a few minutes as much carbonate of soda as we could pile on two large tin plates. This I ground in a coffee mill, and found it nearly pure. We used it in our batter cakes and bread, and found it first rate. Loads of it could be collected in some low places, on the plains, which are white with its efflorescence. The Pimos and Coco Maricopas, had followed us to this camp, and were ready to trade with us for their provisions.

We had been notified that it was forty-five miles to the next water. After watering our animals, which I notice at such times drink heartily as if anticipating a drought, we left camp, at half past five in the afternoon. We generally chose to make the jornadas as much as possible in the night, to avoid the scorching sun. For several miles we were ascending a gentle grade, where the wagon wheels cut deep into the sand which made it extremely laborious for the mules. The track leads away from the river, over a desert, to avoid a bend, with mountains scattered promiscuously around it. At dark we commenced passing through fields of the gigantic cactus, (cerus giganteus). This species of the cactus grows from ten to thirty feet high. Many of them are a single shaft, fluted regularly, and from a foot to eighteen inches in diameter, without a leaf or branch. Directly at the top they produce a fruit more delicious than the fig. Some have branches, from one to six in number, springing from the sides. I observed several specimens, whose branches six in number, grew regularly in the form of chandelier. Their naked trunks, seen by moonlight, scattered over the ground, reminded us the monuments of the dead, and a friend remarked that it seemed as though we were passing a magnificent grave yard. I first observed this species of the cactus a day or two before arriving at Teuson. Several other species rise ten or fifteen feet high, but small. The prickly pear species grow largest lower in Mexico, where it attains an enormous size. The gigantic cactus where grown but a little out of the ground, contains a liquid which is good to quench thirst, and is often useful to the famishing traveler crossing these deserts. It is not found, however, on the largest deserts which we crossed. There is no other vegetation but the larrea, which is very offensive, so that mules prefer eating dry sticks, and some scattered acacias.

JUNE 9TH. At three o'clock in the morning we dropped down into the sand, having tied our animals, by fastening six or eight of their lariats together, so that they might not run away, there not being a spire of grass, and scarcely a shrub near. We slept till five o'clock, when we resumed our journey. Sleep is so oppressive while passing these long jornadas by night overcome by the intense heat of the sun by day, that I cannot refrain from sleeping upon my mule. In the morning we passed down the slope of a mountain where I saw some horns of the mountain goat, and again came into the valley of the Gila, which bore the appearance of former cultivation, and arrived at the river at 12 in the morning. Its water was most grateful to us, after drinking the saline water since leaving the Pimos. The Doctor occasionally shoots birds from which we have some fine stews. Here are the remains of an old zequia, and broken pottery. The valley is wide, and shows evident marks of cultivation. Distance from our last camp about fifty miles.

JUNE 10TH. We were told that we should not strike the river again in less than forty miles, but having traveled ten miles, and coming to a fork in the road, the wagons took that which led to a camping place on the river, and likewise the night being very dark, we concluded to stop until morning. Before arriving, one of the wagons capsized, but did but little damage. This is the first occurrrence of the kind. Before night we met an Irish sailor and two Mexicans, coming up from the river. They stated that they belonged to a party of fifty Mexicans, with one hundred and thirty mules, that were just from Mazatlan, to which place they went for the purpose of taking shipping, but that it was impossible to get passage, on account of the great number of persons waiting there; that they had crossed the country, mountains and deserts, went four days without finding water, took the nearest course to the Gila, through a tap in the mountains, got into the road, and reached the river this afternoon.

JUNE 11TH. Passing down the river at a mile distant,—its course being indicated by a line of cottonwoods, and running under a mountain on the opposite side, while on this side a plain extends two or three miles to some mountains—at 10 o'clock perceiving that we were about to leave the river, we stopped to refresh our animals. There was, however, no grass to be found. Dr. Field and myself taking our water bags and gourds, set out for the river. The sun reflected from the sand, produced a burning heat. We found it more than a mile to water. The river was at this place a quarter of a mile wide. The volume of water at times must be immense, as there is brush and other substances lodged in the mesquites from ten to twenty feet high, through the adjoining plain, over which we have been traveling. Leaving at 4 o'clock, we ascended a bluff to the table lands, covered with black basalt, some of them filled with holes and showing the action of fire. They are heavy and ring like iron. On the left is a range of dark hills, stretching away to the south. Passing over these barren high grounds for several miles, at sundown, we came to a large mass of dark colored granite at the summit, consisting of large blocks loosely thrown together, with plane surfaces. Many of them are four or five feet square. The surface of several of them are covered with hieroglyphics, the work of some ancient people. There was the serpent, lizard, the mastodon, elk, and other animals; also the sun, and many other characters which I could not decipher; one I noticed that resembled a labyrinth or perhaps the streets of a city.

There were two flat rocks with a number of holes which appear to have been used to grind corn, or perhaps to prepare medicine, considerably worn. A few rods beyond we left the old trail of Gen. Kearney. As our advance party had found the road, as it approached the river six miles distant, impassable, we followed the track of Mr. Noble, who was a few weeks before us. At dark we fortunately found a little patch of grass in a small hollow, among some willows, and were very glad to encamp on it.

JUNE 12TH. We took our way over undulating ground, covered with loose black basalt, the ground being light, like dust, into which the wheels sunk, making it hard traveling. This table-land is the most dreary that can well be imagined. At 10, we came near the the river again, and struck the old trail. Looking for a place to water my mule, I found the bank 40 or 50 feet high and very steep, composed of large black blocks, which rest on carbonate of lime, which easily washes away, and precipitates the huge masses into the bed of the stream below. In some places it has left immense perpendicular walls, composed of square blocks of stone, several feet in diameter, as smooth and regular as mason work, far surpassing in grandeur any work of man.

Following the old trail back half a mile, we descended into the bed of the river by a very steep path. The stream, as its present stage, does not occupy more than one-fourth of the bottom; the remainder consists of a deep bed of sand, baked so hard and cracked so deep, that it was difficult to ascertain the depth of the fissures. Going on, we crossed a deep ravine, through which at some seasons runs a large stream. Shortly after we descended the table-land into the river bottom. The banks here are low, and the land fertile, covered with alluvial soil from the overflowing of the river, with scattered heaps of drift-wood and a heavy crop of weeds, but no grass.

We here found an old camp and two U.S. wagons, the parts laying strewn about, a blacksmith's bellows and a quantity of coal. A few miles below we camped on the river, but found nothing but weeds for our animals.

JUNE 13TH. The Governor and company for the first time having neglected to place a guard over the animals, this morning about 20 were missing, and among them my mule. Having searched in every direction, most of them were found by 10 o'clock, six miles down the river; meantime the wagons moved on five miles and camped, where there were a few scattering bunches of grass. I had spent the morning up the river, searching for my mule, and then went down one mile, where I found a camp of Mexicans, who informed me that animals were heard passing their camp during the night. Our company coming up, I borrowed a horse and returned to our old camp for my baggage. On my return I met Dr. Field with my mule, much to my satisfaction. We proceeded a few miles farther and coming to a little dry grass, stopped for those out looking for mules to come up. Being ready at 3 o'clock, moving down the river, we passed the end of a bluff, composed of large blocks of granite, which projected nearly to the river, on which were chiseled some inscriptions in Spanish, in large characters, also some hieroglyphics. A mile below, finding a little spot of excellent grass on the river, we camped. As the bank was high and perpendicular, we drew water with buckets fastened to ropes. There is much complaint among the men, that the Governor travels too slowly in order to recruit his animals, but they cannot justly blame him, as we often go three or four days almost without grass. Distance 8 miles.

JUNE 14TH. I stood on guard last night, for the first time since my lameness; our course to-day, for ten miles, lay through the rich river bottoms, which are occasionally overflowed, leaving a rich deposit of mud. We passed through thousands of acres of wild sun-flowers (?) which grow high and closely set, and bear the appearance of cultivated fields. The flower somewhat resembles the sun-flower with us, being about three inches in diameter; a narrow growth of cottonwoods line the river; flowers of various kinds and brilliant colors are abundant. Of birds, the turtle doves are numerous, their cooings are heard from all quarters. In the river are ducks, geese and swans. Large flocks of small birds, which we call the California quail, are seen running among the weeds, and under the flood-wood. Rising a high bluff and going ten miles over an arid plain, we again came down to the river and camped. We saw several deserted government wagons strewn along the way.

While crossing the table-lands, turning my eye towards the summit of the mountains, on the north side of the river, I called the attention of a comrade to see a city; the basaltic blocks rise in various fantastic shapes. At this place they have the appearance of a city, with its dome, spires and towers, more exactly than any one can imagine. There is, among others, the Capitol at Washington exactly; the beautiful illusion vanished as we proceeded, and assumed other forms.

A Mr. Smith who had gone back to the Pimos village to recover his horse and mule that had strayed away, reported the Pimos and Coco Maricopas returned from a short excursion against the Apaches while he was there, with thirty scalps and two prisoners.[6] He saw a negro and Spaniard who had deserted from our company. Distance, 25 miles.

JUNE 15TH. We first found the mesquite producing their beans. Some of the company collected them for their mules which are very fond of them. When ripe, the pods contain a sweep mucilaginous substance, which is of a pleasant taste. Saw more abandoned wagons. On approach to the river, the ground is covered with a saline efflorescence.

We collected some salt, of good quality, from the steep banks of the river. At 12 o'clock we found a little grass among the sunflowers, and stopped to give our mules a bite; the wagons moved on. At 5, the doctor and myself went forward a few miles and found a little grass under the branches of some mesquites, which we pulled for our animals. The wagons not coming up, we camped by ourselves for the night.

JUNE 16TH. At daylight the doctor started back to the wagons to attend to his loose animals that ran in the caballada, and having warmed some penole, which was the only thing I happened to have with me for supper and breakfast, I went on alone in search of grass for my mule.

At the distance of six miles the trail took me to the river, where I watered my mule. On leaving the river, he suddenly plunged into a hole of quicksand, and if he had not acted in the emergency with that degree of intelligence and judgment which is not generally attributed to brutes, his journey might have ended here. Hastily tearing off his saddle, I extended his fore feet to firmer ground, where he kept them planted as I wished, and when I had made him ready, and lent a hand to assist, and gave him the word to start, he strained every muscle, without flouncing, to extricate his hind quarters which were gradually sinking in the mire. After a few efforts he succeeded, although afterwards he was so exhausted and in such a tremor, as scarcely to be able to move for several minutes; I then took him to the river and gave him a nice washing. I have on several other occasions observed, that he was not so stupid as his long ears would seem to indicate. I found a little bunch of grass under the steep banks, which I pulled for him. The wagons came up in a few hours.

Commencing to cross another sand plain, we again went forward of the wagons to look for grass, and discovered a few scattered bunches on low sandy ground near the river, which, with considerable labor, we cut as usual, and again camped for the night. The wagon mules not being able to get to grass fared badly.

JUNE 17TH. The wagons coming up at seven, we went on, following the river until 12 o'clock, when we camped within six miles of the passage of the river through the mountains. Today we first felt sensibly the delightful and refreshing breeze from the direction of the Pacific. We have, for several days past, found a small berry which has dried upon its bushes, six or eight feet high, which we pick from our saddles whenever we have an opportunity. They have a fine flavor.

JUNE 18TH. Last night it being my turn to guard the animals, the sergeant informed me, as I was preparing supper, that they were at the right of the watering place, which was one fourth of a mile distant from the wagons. I started at dark, supposing it was but a short distance, and followed their trail down the river in the darkness, two miles, through the tall sunflowers and weeds, with occasionally a water-hole in the sand, directed the last part of the way by the watch-fires, and arrived pretty well exhausted, as I had walked in the sand considerably in the afternoon to favor my mule. I was relieved from duty at 10, and rather than undertake to return in the darkness, I crept under a part of a blanket of a neighbor upon a sand-bank, and slept until morning. There is hardly a possibility of taking cold in this climate, the air is so dry and the ground so warm. This morning we had a fatiguing march along the sandy river bottom, and at 12 o'clock we stopped, where there was no grass, to rest the teams.

These plains are composed of sand with iron pyrites, and salt; there is a little scattered sage and larrea Mexicana.

JUNE 19. Passing among sand and gravel hills along the bends of the river; stopping to water our animals at the river, some of them became mired in the quicksand and were with difficulty saved. Three or four Indians made their appearance; they had no clothing but an old rag, and wished to beg every mouthful of food they could see. I gave two of them some hard bread and they followed me to get more, rubbing their shriveled maws to signify their famishing condition. We soon after met a dozen more, men and women, going up the river, with baskets on their heads, to gather the beans of the mesquite, which they make much use of; they are altogether the most miserable race of beings I ever saw. Dr. Scott, one of the company from Mississippi, lost a fine horse at our camp near the Pimos village. His negro man went back but could not find him. This morning a man belonging to a late company came up with him; he had found him on the field of grass where we camped. He was not willing to give him up, until after considerable contention and some threats, but seeing our strength, and the spirit of the doctor, he promised to deliver him at the Colerado. Coming again into deep sand, the Governor stopped to rest his mules. After dinner, Drs. Field and Brent, of Mississippi, and myself, went on and found a little grass upon a steep back of the old channel of the river, which we cut for our animals. We watered them at some pools of stagnant water, left by the receding river. Dr. Brent undertook to go to the river for water for himself, but after a hard tramp of nearly two miles he gave it up. As we expected the wagons to pass by the road, which we supposed one and a half miles distant, at 4 we started out, and had to make our way through a dense field of sunflowers, generally eight or ten feet high, with great fatigue to ourselves and animals. Standing upon our mules to take observations occasionally, we could see nothing but one vast field of sunflowers and the mountains in the distance; but taking a direct course, and laying our hand upon the necks of our mules, to keep them clear of the dense growth, the strongest taking the lead, they finally broke a passage to the road. The company coming up, we proceeded through these fields, several miles to an old camp, with ruins of wagons, probably Graham's,[7] beyond which we turned off the trail a mile or two, and sent our animals to grass.

I took my canteens and gourds and started for water, leaving the doctor to cook supper. Passing through the grass meadow, where was a Mexican camp, I came to a pond a mile beyond. I got back to camp after dark, much fatigued, but was refreshed by an excellent supper, consisting of birds killed during the day, penole pudding and coffee. A man returned who had gone before to the Colorado and stated the distance at 18 miles, the river within its banks, and other information which was cheering to us, as it had been reported that the river was impassable.

JUNE 20TH. Passing down the river, we arrived among some sand and gravel hills, upon one of which a part of us ascended and beheld the junction of the famed Colerado and Gila. Below the junction they pass through a cañon [canyon] about one fourth of a mile long, and with walls 50 feet high. On the north side, the mountains rise with several remarkable looking prominences, one of which resembles a round tower. With some difficulty the wagons were brought to the banks of the Colerado one and a half miles below the junction. There is a thick growth of willows and cotton-woods, filled up with canes, vines, and weeds along the bank, through which it is difficult to penetrate. Farther back are clusters of mesquite; there was a road cut through the thicket to the river. We hastened down to look at this celebrated stream which we had long wished to see. It is, at its present stage, within its banks and falling rapidly.

From appearances, it seldom overflows at this point. It is about 350 yards wide, its current deep and strong, and its waters of a deep yellow color, from the clay and mud it carries with it. The waters of the Gila are clear and sea green. There is no grass near the crossing on the Mexican side, but the Indians (Yumas) who throng the camp, bring the stalks of the young cane from the other side, which is considered nearly as good as grass for the animals. These Indians being fine formed, athletic, and excellent swimmers, ven-tured across the stream with their bundles of cane, but it is a difficult feat, as the current carries them down half a mile before they can reach the bank. I have never heard of an American at-tempting to swim across here.

The Colerado is said to be navigable to this place for large steamboats, and at no distant day we may look for a city here which will be the emporium of the extensive hunting, grazing, agricul-tural and mineral country above.[8] Near the junction, on the north side, are the ruins of a Spanish church; it was built by Father Kino about 250 years ago, but the settlement was finally depopulated by the Indians.

ACROSS THE GREAT DESERT
TO CARRIZO CREEK AND OJO GRANDE

June 21 – July 1, 1849

JUNE 21ST. There is a party of Mexicans a few rods from us, also an American company with whom are Morris and Burke of our original company.

The American company are engaged this morning in crossing their animals; the current is so swift, that they float down half a mile before they can land on the opposite side; they employ Indians to conduct them; each holds a mule by the bridle, swimming before. I saw one fine mule drowned; a party that had crossed day before yesterday had five drowned. Jordan's company had five mules stolen. The Humas Indians are good looking, well proportioned fellows, but they are treacherous and not to be trusted. Our company are making two boats to cross their goods in. Their frames are made of willow poles, in shape of a ship's boat, and covered with India rubber blankets. Five mules have been drowned today. Only 25 or 30 have crossed safely.

JUNE 22D. The Indians have some money, but do not know the true value of it, hence we suppose they have robbed some travelers. An Indian offered a gold quarter eagle for a peck of beans, another a half, for two quarts of corn, and another a quarter eagle for a quart of beans. They have some mules which can be purchased for a red blanket a-piece. There are some scorpions and tarantulas about the camp; they are ugly, poisonous creatures.

JUNE 23D. The company having completed a boat, made two trips with her this afternoon. She is 18 feet long and shaped like a whaleboat. The others are about the same size. In crossing, the current carries the boat down stream, and in returning a little more distance is added in spite of the most active rowing; we are obliged to bring it up to the starting point on our shoulders, which is a laborious operation. The Governor has sent his animals a few miles up the river to grass.[1]

JUNE 24TH. We have been all day in getting our animals and goods across the river; we had crossed all, excepting two, without the loss of any; we adopted the Texian plan of leading one or two on each side of the boat.

It is surprising to see with what ease the Indians swim the rapid current. I saw one swim with his foot under the chin of a drowning mule and save him.[2]

JUNE 25TH. We have all got over, and camped at the landing among thick cottonwoods and tall weeds, which we have cut away and formed comfortable stalls for our animals, and places for ourselves in the shade. Nothing can be more delightful, we need no better shelter. Dr. Field, Dr. Rice, and myself went out, two miles on the plains, in the morning, to graze our animals; we found down the river some cane and plenty of pig-weeds, but no grass.

The greater part of Mexico through which we have passed, consists of dry table land, with but few streams of water, and many of these, although torrents in the wet season, are dry for a considerable part of the year. High and precipitous mountains rise in every direction, destitute of vegetation, and, in many places, form impassable barriers to communication. The whole of this table land is destitute of timber suitable for building, and what sticks can be procured for rafters and other necessary purposes are crooked staddles, and would, in most countries, be rejected as useless. On account of the want of water the settlements are far between, although where the land can be irrigated it produces large crops. There are a few beautiful valleys whose climate and soil will compare favorably with any in the world, yet from want of communication with the sea, *produce* for exploration cannot be raised with profit. On account of the scarcity of water, there are but few birds or insects, and the atmosphere is so very dry, that meat will keep for a considerable length of time without salt.

This country, both from its nature and the character of the

Clarke's trail through California

people, can be of no use as an appendage to any other country. The people generally are evidently not sufficiently enlightened, and are too liable to become dupes to partisan chiefs, to be able to support for any length of time a stable, independent government. As a whole, the central part cannot be considered a desirable country.

JUNE 26TH. The greater part of the company have concluded to leave the wagons, as their progress is very slow, and there is no longer much danger of the Indians. The doctor and myself having made preparations, placed ourselves in the company of some Mexicans, and went down the river to a watering place, not far from the ford. We found here Dr. Scott and about a dozen others.

There was not much for the animals, but a kind of pig-weed, which the mules eat greedily. We carefully collected all the grass we could find, as we felt that their lives were nearly as important as ours, as ours might depend upon theirs in crossing the great desert before us. There was at this place an encampment of Jumas [Yumas]; they were collecting and preparing mesquite beans, of which they make molasses, and use in various ways: also the seed of the weed before mentioned. These they dry in the chaff, then beat them out, and grind them upon a metate and make them into a porridge.

The dress of the women consisted of a frill of bark, fastened by a band around the loins, otherwise entirely unencumbered. But though their dress was of as brief a pattern as that of Mother Eve, they appeared also as modest as she. There was among them one girl, who appeared to be the belle, and might be called handsome, which I think very uncommon among Indian women. The captain, or chief, was among them; he speaks Spanish. Capt. Allen of St. Louis and two others were drowned, in crossing the river near here a short time since. Eleven of us being ready two hours before sundown, we started upon the desert without a guide, and with no certain knowledge of its features. This desert is more than a hundred miles across, with no water, except in holes dug in the ground at two or three places, and these often get filled up with sand. We hastened down the river, over difficult hills of sand and gravel, twelve or fourteen miles. At dark the path had diverged from the river considerably; looking down a steep bank we saw two fires; we hailed their proprietors, but no answer being returned we kept on. Turning directly from the river, we entered upon the sand-drifts;[3]

we dismounted from our animals, and commenced wading through these banks, which in form and cleanliness gave the scene the appearance of a northern mid-winter night, although the warm breezes were fanning our exposed chests. After a few hours of hard labor, we left the sand-hills, and entered upon a hard plain, covered with scattered pieces of lava. As the moon went down, we tied our animals to some mesquite bushes, and laid down in the sand to repose.

JUNE 27TH. We rose at daylight, and having taken a hasty breakfast, started on to reach the first well, which was 36 miles from the river, before it became too hot. Stopping to give our animals some mesquite beans, we arrived at a dry arroyo at 8 o'clock. Rushing into it, we found a hole eight feet deep, with a dead horse and a few inches of water at the bottom. We found another a little farther up the gully, in the same condition. Some of us were nearly out of water, and knew not how far it was to the next, but we determined to press on. Going up the arroyo, I saw several dead animals with their saddles and trappings.

We soon came to an extensive plain of sand, with no green thing but a shrub which even a mule will sooner die than eat. The day was extremely hot, and some of us being nearly out of water, dare only wet our mouths; our sufferings from thirst were great. Early in the afternoon, we passed a large wagon, which had been abandoned by Mr. Noble, with the harnesses, cooking utensils, &c., scattered about. Some of us stopped to rest awhile in its shade, others kept on. The doctor and myself stopped in the afternoon and fixed a blanket upon the largest bush we could find to afford a little shade. Our animals munched what dry sticks they could find greedily.

Mr. Smith from New Orleans coming up, leading his mule, we hailed him and asked if he had any water, to which he replied, not a drop, and showed us his tongue, saying he was famishing. Starting on with him on foot, we met a poor old horse that had been left by some one. He looked at us a little and staggered on. We saw more than a dozen dead animals with their trappings on the road to-day.

When any one saw a saddle better than his own, he made an exchange. After dark, the rear came up, and we moved slowly over a sand-hill, with fearful forebodings, and as the moon had not yet risen, we found it difficult to keep the trail.

Such as these, are times to try men's souls. Some broke out in the most extravagant expressions, declaring that we had lost the way—should never find water,—all perish, &c. Others said nothing, but jogged steadily on, with a fixed determination to persevere. After traveling an hour or two more, we came suddenly to the brow of a steep sand-bank, and saw fires beneath us. We all shouted; some asking if there was any water, to which the reply was—yes, if you can wait for it. Going down the steep bank, we encountered a horrid stench arising from dead animals which lay around; tying the mules to prevent them from falling into the wells, I soon found one of these holes, which was twelve or fourteen feet deep.[4] Letting myself down by a stick which lay across the top, I found a little muddy water at the bottom, which I dipped up with my tin cup. Never did water taste more sweet. I then filled two gourds, which I carried up and stirred penole into it, and drank about two quarts, until I was satisfied. Some of the company declared they drank a gallon, and I do not doubt it, although I should have done so before this experience. (This had a sweetish taste; that of the other well at which the animals were watered is brackish.) We then proceeded to water our animals. We dipped with a tin cup into a pail, and emptied into an Indian rubber keeler, out of which the animals drank. There is danger of the sand caving in; four of us labored until 10 o'clock at night, and I rose before light that I might have an opportunity to fill my vessels.

JUNE 28TH. We took our animals out two miles to eat mesquite beans, which fortunately are plenty at that place at this time, or the poor brutes would have left their bones on this desert. We returned at 11 o'clock, wishing to water again in the afternoon and start on our journey, but another company coming up, we were obliged, through courtesy, to wait till an hour before sundown, when we gave them as much as they wanted. Mr. Noble had sent a message back, and had stuck notices upon some wagons which he had left here, that it was eleven leagues to the next well, the water of which was so bad as to kill all animals that drank it; and 60 miles through to the water of Carrizo Creek. Dr. Field and myself therefore filled what vessels we had, and also an India rubber pillow, and went on by moonlight. At 2 o'clock, we lay down by the path and slept until morning.

JUNE 29TH. Starting at light, we soon came to some mesquites, and gave our animals a breakfast. I then went forward, till about noon, when we found more beans and gathered them for our animals. Two Mexicans who passed us last night returned from the well, three miles ahead, and stopped with us. Two hours before sundown we proceeded to the well which is located in a deep hollow. The water was salt and very offensive, but we gave our animals a little. In the night we passed over large tracts of land as barren of any kind of vegetation as a brick-yard, upon which the hoofs of our animals made no impression. The smooth surface of the ground glittered in the moonbeams. In order to relieve my mule, I walked about one half of the way, as I have often done. With one hand hold of the horn of the saddle, we have jogged along together many a weary mile. Sleep and weariness became very oppressive, as this was the fourth night since we had had much rest. Two hours before day, we stopped in the sand and slept about an hour.

JUNE 30TH. We arrived at Carrizo (Cane) Creek at noon; this is the first running water on this side of the desert. The whole distance, we have passed carcasses of mules and horses, particularly at the end of the route; I should judge at least 30 or 40 a day. A short distance back, we passed a poor mule with a saddle on, standing in the path, while a pack of wolves were howling for him over a neighboring sand-hill. The creek can be stepped over in some places, and disappears in the sand, a mile below. The last part of the journey on the desert is the most forlorn that can be imagined, consisting of immense sand-hills, worn into various singular shapes, outskirting the desert with mica, and layers of gypsum. As there is no grass here, we went on hoping to find some. Driving through the sand up the shallow bed of the quondam stream in the scorching sun, we stopped at 3 o'clock, not being able to find grass. The animals eat a few leaves from some of the miserable bushes. An hour before sundown we proceeded up the mountains; at 10 o'clock we met two Indians, who told us that there was plenty of grass, and an encampment of Americans a short distance ahead. We soon came to it, and were again delighted with the sight of grass; we had not seen a spire for four days. Several of the company have lost animals on the desert.

JULY 1ST. There are about half a dozen Indian huts here, the most miserable that can be imagined, merely sheds four or five feet high, covered with cane and reeds and open on one or two sides. There is here a bold and beautiful sulphur spring, called Ojo Grande, forming a magnificent pool, 15 or 20 feet in diameter, the waters of which have a fine medicinal taste; also several smaller ones of pure water. These are the source of Carrizo Creek.

THROUGH WARNER'S AND WILLIAMS' RANCHES
TO PUEBLO-DE-LOS-ANGELOS

July 2—10, 1849

JULY 2D. Numbers of our rear, and the forerunners of the Mexican company arriving, we resumed our journeyings. Passing through the valley, we crossed over a narrow ridge of mountains, and found ourselves in another valley, apparently entirely mountain-locked; however, following the track, it led us into a very remarkable defile, that opened in the side of the mountain. This pass is so narrow, as only to give room for a road. On either side are high, and most of the way precipitous rocks for nearly two miles. The bottom is sandy and as smooth as a plain. A stream of water evidently runs down this passage in the rainy season, and has thus left a sandy bottom. At one place the pass between the perpendicular rocks is only about four feet wide, and, of course, wagons to pass, must be taken to pieces. Mr. Noble, from Chihuahua, passed about two weeks since, besides which probably no more than one or two trains ever passed. The rocks on either side have been broken off, probably by Maj. Graham or Mr. Noble. Winding our way for several miles among mountains, some of which are said to be 5,000 feet high, we came to a little Indian settlement of San Felippe. It consists of perhaps twenty or thirty huts and sheds. The Indians cultivate a few vegetables. We had for supper a fine rabbit stew. Dr. Field and myself being alone, we again packed up a little after dark, and coming upon a plain, soon found ourselves upon the wrong trail. We have entered the grass country of California, the oaks begin to have the appearance of trees; becoming convinced that we were wrong, after following a cattle track some distance, I took a straight course across the plain, and about half a mile distant found the road and gave notice to my companion by hallooing. We camped at 12 o'clock at night, the weather very cool, so that we found it necessary to use our overcoats or blankets. We had got upon high grounds; we passed on the way through thickets of the agave Americana, the centennial plant; the sharp thorns at the ends of the leaves are very annoying.

JULY 3D. Two Indians visited us this morning, and informed us that we were within two leagues of a mission and five or six from Warner's Rancheria. Crossing a mountain of several miles we came in view of an extensive valley; crossing a part of it, we ascended a hill, where we were met by about a dozen Indians well dressed and mounted on fine fat horses; they informed us that Warner's was over the hill. We arrived at noon; it comprises a fine valley of considerable extent. The various kinds of grasses were abundant, and of fine quality. Warner was not at home, much to our disappointment, as we were expecting to obtain information and provisions of him. Mr. Warner is from Middletown, Conn.[1] I was informed afterwards that he had been gone for months. The Aqua Callienta [Agua Caliente] (hot sprints) at this place I have since been told are of the temperature of 137° Fahrenheit. The predominant mineral is sulphur.[2]

Provisions are exorbitantly high, it being the first rancho in California, and travelers arriving from a long distance, and where there is but little opportunity for purchasing food, are sometimes scandalously imposed upon. For beef, they asked as high as 20 or 25 cents per pound; horses nearly as high as in the States. Two years ago they could be bought for from five to fifteen dollars. There are three small vineyards here that look well. In the afternoon, going on we entered among the hills, from whose tops we could see the level lawns of the valley, with its luxuriant grass and groves of oak that grow in long narrow strips through the valley, forming a fine landscape. We camped among the mountains at 10 o'clock. The mountains are beginning to cover their nakedness considerably.

JULY 4TH. We passed several Indian settlements. About noon we met two Indians, from whom we succeeded in purchasing three dollars worth of jerked beef. They sell it by the bundle. They cooked some beef and asked us to eat. I thought it the most delicious I ever tasted. They were returning from Pueblo-de-los-

Angelos, and displayed some handkerchiefs, and other dry goods, which they had purchased, and the prices paid. The merchants will get rich there if they have large sales. We camped in a beautiful valley, thirty miles from the Aqua Callienta, holding thousands of acres of the best grass land. After a long parley we succeeded in purchasing a small sheep; the price first named was $10; we finally paid $2. Dr. Scott's party of six, were with us.

JULY 5TH. Passing over a succession of hills, we came to a valley where was a rancho with a solitary house, and as usual a corral, formed by stakes driven into the ground, for the cattle. Large herds of cattle and goats were grazing on the plain; the cattle are of a superior quality. We camped at night under a large willow, at the end of a beautiful lake two or three miles long. The moon appearing in the heavens, shedding her mild rays into the tranquil water, while clumps of cottonwoods, at intervals along the shores relieved the mind from the idea of barrenness, to which we have been long accustomed, together with low ranges of mountains at no great distance, formed an enchanting scene. We sat down to our supper of veal stew by the moonlight. I know not by what name this lake is known, but I shall call it Lake Bonita.

JULY 6TH. We passed several ranchos, well stocked with cattle. The inhabitants live almost exclusively on meat; they are called beef ranchos. No flour or other provisions are to be had.[3] We are living in their style, from necessity.

JULY 7TH. We have been passing through large fields of mustard growing wild, which was nearly ripe and fit to cut. It appears like our American mustard, and grows rank and thick. A little before noon we came to Williams' rancho. Col. Williams has a wheat mill with one run of stone, which he is obliged to keep running night and day to supply travelers. The flour is unbolted. We bought an alimuer, about six quarts for one dollar. He raises large crops without irrigation. The neighboring hills are covered to their tops with wild oats, which were ripe. They are as free from grass and weeds as our cultivated fields. We turned our mules into them and rested at noon. I saw here some wagons, and other indications of civilized life. The California cart, their only carriage, is a most clumsy thing. Its wheels are composed of a transverse section of a tree, and but a little more than two feet in diameter. Some of them have a roof, made of hides, which are their pleasure carriages. Colonel Williams offered Mr. Evans, of Pa., who is with us, fifty cents for every fanega, or two bushels of wheat he would grind in his mill. When in order, it would grind two fanegas in an hour. He has from ten to fifteen thousand head of neat cattle, besides a large number of horses. [4]

JULY 8TH. We remained among the oats until afternoon, when we moved six miles over the hills and again camped. One of the Dr's mules being lame, he stopped to doctor it. These hills are all covered with wild oats. I am becoming very impatient at the slow progress we are making, and at the long, unexpectedly long, and ever lengthening journey. The comforts of social life, and the endearments of home never seemed so precious to me before.

JULY 9TH. Mustard on the plains, and oats on the hills, again, to-day. We passed in the morning, several large ruined buildings, but did not learn what they were. Arriving at Pueblo-de-los-Angelos, (city of the angels,) we as usual made our camp on some grass in the suburbs. [5] We called in the afternoon at a rancho, where we purchased some beef of the lady of the house. The meat had been lately jerked, but as we were out of provisions, we commenced eating it, without stopping for it to be cooked. As we were about leaving, she called us back, and gave us a plate of excellent stewed meat, with so much kindness, and grace, that we could not admire the propriety of her behavior, and ease of her manners before strangers; especially as she appeared to be the only person about the premises.

JULY 10TH. There are two routes leading from this place to the mines. One the coast route, five hundred miles, and the other the valley between the coast range and the Sierra Nevada, (snowy mountains,) four hundred miles, which is, in places, destitute of water, at this season of the year. We concluded to take the longest route.

Pueblo-de-los-Angelos is situated twenty-four miles from its *embarcadero* [landing stage] on the Pacific. Within and near the town, the ground is abundantly irrigated from a creek, and is in a good state of cultivation. The buildings are of adobes, but of a better kind than is common in Mexico, and there is more use made of lumber. I met with a number of Americans, who had been in the country a number of years, and were wealthy. I called at the house of a Frenchman, who complained bitterly of the present government. He stated that now he could not get justice done; formerly it was not so. The chief justice of the place owed him $400, for which, he had his note, but he could not get it.

I unexpectedly met with three of my old company. Searles was working at tailoring for a wealthy man; twelve dollars was paid for making a coat, five for a vest, &c. Newland and Hudson were making an adobe wall at one dollar per day and board. They were going to leave for the diggings in a few days. The fare in a sailer to San Francisco was twenty dollars. Leaving town we passed, a few miles out, several places in and near the road, from which were oozing petroleum. I noticed large beds of it that had become hard. The people in town make use of it to cover the tops of the walls that surround their vineyards, gardens, &c. While in the Pueblo, Mr. Cole, of the No. Adams, Mass. company, joined us. He went to Mazatlan with his company, who took shipping from that place, but hearing that mules were worth from three to four hundred dollars at the mines, (which was incorrect), as they were worth but little in Mazatlan, he undertook to conduct those that belonged to his company, by land. When he arrived he had but two animals, all the rest having perished. Three men who traveled a part of the way with him, also perished from thirst. Distance thirty miles.

July 11th—March, 1851

JULY 11TH. Our road this morning carried us among the mountains, which rise in every direction, but we generally avoided them, by winding around. In the afternoon, after descending the Coast Range, one of the most steep and difficult mountains which we have crossed, we found ourselves upon a wide plain, which we were satisfied would extend to the ocean. Seeing a group of good sized birds, within gun shot, I called the attention of the doctor to them. We directly calculated upon a nice stew for supper; he fired, I saw a parcel of them fall over; we ran up, and found that he had killed five owls, that were sitting over the hole of a prairie dog, or some other animal, in which these birds live. About sundown, we met a Mexican, and asked him how far it was to water; he said one league. Going more than two, and not finding any, we turned off to some trees and camped. Of late, we have not let our animals loose, hobbling part of them. If the grass is good they will not wander far from camp. After building a fire, and disposing of our baggage, we first heard a roaring sound, for which a moment we were at a loss to account for, but were immediately satisfied that it proceeded from the surf of the Pacific, apparently four or five miles distant.

The nights have been damp since we have arrived near the ocean, and the fogs do not clear away before eight or nine o'clock in the morning. Distance thirty-eight miles.

JULY 12TH. Calling at a rancho we purchased some meat and milk at reasonable prices. We soon came in sight of what we had long wished to see, the Pacific Ocean. Its wide waves can be observed at a considerable distance, following each other, and gathering force from their long career until they run far upon the beach, and again recede. But still there is a calmness, and quiet grandeur in it, and its whisperings and murmurings seem to speak of hidden things. Our path ran along the beach; the mountains in some places coming to the water's edge. The path was along the steep sides of the mountain, in places overhanging the sea. At others we passed over the sandy beach, the waves sometimes flowing to our animals' feet. Whale bones are scattered along the shore. While stopping to refresh our animals, a drove of fat cattle passed us, going to the mines. At 11 o'clock passed Sante Beneventura [Santa Buenaventura], formerly a flourishing mission, but now decaying. It consists of a very large church, and several long rows of buildings of one story, covered with tiles, situated under a mountain near the sea. There are extensive gardens, surrounded with high adobe walls, which are now beginning to fall. There are some fruit trees; we gathered some pears, which were not ripe. Distance 30 miles.

In July 1831, there were in California 21 missions, to which were attached about 18,000 Indians. These were kept in a state of dependence upon the missions, and were made to cultivate the neighboring grounds, to a considerable extent. In 1833, under the independent government, the salary of the Monks was discontinued, the Indians were released from servitude, and the mission fund confiscated. The missions were soon deserted. Some of them are now in the possession of private individuals. They were built on a grand scale, and some of them with considerable taste.

JULY 13TH. Passing along the "sounding shore," we came to a place where the mountains recede, and there are several ranches that are well cultivated, and very fruitful. The cool breezes from the ocean render it pleasant traveling. Large oaks, with wide spreading gnarled branches, are hung with festoons of lace-like moss.

We stopped a few hours in Sante Barbara. This town is pleasantly situated, and from a distance has the appearance of being larger than it really is. There are but four or five stores, and but little business is done. The best grazing country is from San Diego past this place.

Two vessels were at anchor off the town. One of them from Mazatlan with passengers for San Francisco. It has been 45 days on its way, and stopped for water and provisions. The passengers were from Texas, and some of them had taken a little too much aguardiente, and had committed some excesses. There is one large church.

Common brown sugar sells for 37 ½ cents, and rice from 12 ½ to 18¾ cents per lb. I found it impossible to get any cooking vessels. We have been using some earthen pots which we found on the San Pedro, and a tin pint cup; a pint cup costs a dollar. One of our company paid another dollar for an old coffee pot, minus handle and spout, and whose sides were so knocked in that it would be difficult to describe it by geometrical figures. We camped five miles out of town. The grass is mostly dried up, but the California clover, which is beaten down, affords a large quantity of seed, on which animals fatten. All the horses, as well as cattle, of which I have seen thousands, are fatter than I ever saw before. Distance 25 miles.

JULY 14TH. A herd of horses that were feeding near us got up a stampede in the night, and took one of our mules with them. We passed a valley in the mountains opening to the sea, where there was a very strong smell of petroleum. We did not go out of our way to see from whence it came. Passing along the shore, in the afternoon, we saw a steamship making rapid progress towards the north. We supposed it to be the regular steamer from Panama.

We frequently cross deep ravines which are steep and difficult. They occur between ridges that end in the sea. At night we overtook Mr. Noble, from Chihuahua, with two wagons. He had left four on the route. He was carrying baggage for men going to the mines. His principal object however was to get his mules and wagons there. Distance 30 miles.

JULY 15TH. Following the shore a few hours, we struck off into the mountains, among huge rocks, and scenery of the wildest description. Stopped at a rancho among the mountains, where we obtained some provisions. At conspicuous places in the mountain passes, companies that have preceded us, have written various kinds of information upon the rocks, and the skulls of cattle, that lay by the path. The hills are covered with wild oats.

In the afternoon we stopped at Sante Ines [Santa Ynés], a mission, to obtain information concerning the road. It was similar to others we have seen, enclosed by a strong wall. A few Indians were seen about the premises. There were cells with iron grated windows, about the court. Every thing was on a large scale. We camped among the mountains. Distance 25 miles.

JULY 16TH. Crossing a high and steep mountain, we came to a valley stocked with thousands of cattle, belonging to a rancho at which we arrived at 10 o'clock. As it is a fair specimen of the Spanish ranches in this section, I will give a short sketch of it. The ground in front of the house was strown [strewn] with the offal of cattle, on which scores of buzzards and crows were feeding in quiet security; and, as is commonly the case, the skulls and skeletons of animals, had been allowed to accumulate, making a perfect Golgotha. Nothing was to be had for food, but beef, and hence arises the name of beef ranches. We then crossed a low sand plain 24 miles, and arrived the other side and camped in some clover, before dark. This plain is as level as a floor, nearly destitute of vegetation, and has the appearance of having been the bed of a lake, as there are well defined banks where we entered and left it.

In crossing it I was witness to an optical illusion, which I have often heard described, but never saw before. A little before night, having fallen nearly a mile behind my companions, and looking in the direction of the bank, before me, perhaps six or eight miles distant, the sun being very hot, I saw coming towards me the appearance of a man 20 or 30 feet high. This continued perhaps fifteen minutes, but as we approached each other, the figure gradually diminished to the size of an ordinary man, and proved to be a Mexican whom I met walking alone.

On relating the circumstance when I arrived at our camp, the doctor mentioned an instance which happened in Texas during its

war with Mexico. The inhabitants of a little port were one afternoon thrown into a state of alarm by the appearance of a large vessel
at sea, making its way into the harbor, but were relieved by its
arriving in the size of a small sail-boat before night. Distance 36
miles.

JULY 17TH. We arrived at the Rancho Napoma, kept by an
American, before breakfast, when we obtained milk and penole.
We afterwards again came in view of the sea. There are numerous
small streams of excellent water running from the mountains.
Distance 28 miles.

JULY 18TH. We arrived at San Luis Obispo, the capital of a
county, formerly a state of that name. The mission buildings are in
the shape of a large compact square, and with a few other buildings, form a small village. They are occupied by Indians and
Mexicans. There is one variety store, and several grog shops. Flour
12½ cents, and sugar 50 cents per lb. There was a proclamation
posted up, issued by Gov. Riley, setting forth the existing form of
government in California, and calling for a general convention on
the first of September, and also ordering the election of the alcaldes
in the different departments of the state, &c.

There were camped near here forty soldiers, on their way north,
to quell the Indians, who are making attacks on small parties, and
have killed eight Americans. We camped three miles from San
Luis.

JULY 19TH. We remained in camp. Oats are plenty, and we find
it necessary to recruit our animals. Several parties have passed,
returning from the mines. It is reported that foreigners are ordered
to leave the mines within a month. We have been meeting parties
for several days past.

JULY 20TH. We left the camp early, and crossed the mountain
into a valley, where at a rancho we saw an American soldier who
had been wounded in a dispute, by an officer. Upon a mountain we
saw the first pines since entering Mexico. At noon we stopped at a
deserted rancho, where a company of dragoons were encamped

with wagons. They were engaged in burning a coal pit, and were probably preparing to shoe their horses. Temple and Rice, of the North Adams company, joined us. Distance 28 miles.

JULY 21ST. A company camped near, killed a deer, and gave us half of it. Passed a large sulphur spring. At noon we stopped at the deserted mission, San McGill [San Miguel]. Distance 28 miles.

JULY 22D. Five of our animals straying off last night, it was 10 o'clock before we were ready to start this morning. They were found about five miles from our camp. We have come to white oaks here; the oaks heretofore have been of a species which grow eight or ten feet, and extend their wide spreading branches. The trunks of some are five or six feet in diameter. They now begin to run up higher, and are better adapted for building timber. We passed a grizzly bear and cubs, that had been killed, in the road. Saw an animal which we supposed to be that called a Mexican lion, and were waked at night by the roaring of animals which we supposed to be the same. Our mules were terribly frightened, but we prevented them from breaking away. Rabbits and deer, and other game are plenty. Distance 16 miles.

JULY 23RD. Soon after starting, we passed a rancho, where we obtained meat and milk, and at 11 o'clock we arrived at San Antonio, a mission now deserted, but whose extensive buildings and fields, walled in with adobes, with drains for irrigation, are proofs of its former prosperity. Crossing a steep mountain, in the afternoon, we camped on the farther side, where we found wild oats. Distance 30 miles.

JULY 24TH. Coming down the mountain side, we saw several herds of deer. Towards night we came to a little deserted village, called Colora, where a Mexican, probably from Monterey, had established himself in a vacant room with a few things, principally eatables, to sell to travelers. He asked 50 cents for sugar, 25 cents for rice, and 12 ½ cents for a loaf of bread containing two mouthfuls; we did not purchase. Distance 30 miles.

JULY 25TH. Starting without water, we went till one o'clock

without finding any. We stopped at a deserted rancho, where we found water, and camped on a grassy spot. We have left Monterey to the left, and go by the mission of St. John [San Juan], (pronounced in Spanish San Whan), it being a nearer way to the first mines. JULY 26TH. We overtook a young Frenchman, resident of St. Johns, in the morning, on his way from Monterey. He was very communicative, and gave us considerable information concerning the mines and its vicinity. We arrived at St. Johns, formerly a mission. The buildings are now otherwise tenanted. There are a few stores and hotels, and one or two American families. After procuring some provisions, much lower than we had previously paid, and getting some pears from the fine and extensive old mission garden, we camped at the farther side of a wide plain, near a rancho, called Pachecqua Pass, eight miles from St. Johns. Distance to San Francisco one hundred miles; from Stanislaus eighty miles. The reports from the mines are, that some get large quantities of gold, others but little. As a specimen of the bravery of the Mexicans, I will relate what was communicated by Mr. Cole. On his way from Mazatlan, he came upon five Mexican soldiers, who belonged to a company stationed among the mountains, to look out for robbers that infest the road. They were at a hut where were four other Mexicans. Before he left the hut, he noticed a gun and pistol, belonging to a member of his company, lying on the ground, and mentioned to the owner that he had better look out or the Mexicans would steal his arms; but was answered, not very pleasantly, that he would take care of his arms. They had gone about two miles when the man overtook them, saying that he believed the Mexicans had stolen his gun and pistol, as he could not find them. They did not feel very pleasantly about turning back, as it was very warm, and the man had shown great carelessness; notwithstanding, he, the interpreter, and two other men started back, and met four of the troops on the road. Cole went directly up to one of them, and giving him a pretty severe shaking, ordered him to vamos [go] directly back to the hut with him, and give him his gun and pistol, or he would shoot every one of them, at the same time drawing his revolver.

When they had returned to the hut, they all denied, at first, that they knew any thing about the arms, but after some management, he got possession of their weapons, and placed a man over them with his pistol cocked.

Two of them then started down a gully, where one of them hid himself and was seen no more. The other presently appeared at the top of a hill, holding up the gun to show that he had found it. Cole motioned him to come with it, which he did, saying that the other man that was missing, stole the gun. Cole upon that, gave him a few knocks, upon which the fellow pretended to be killed, but upon applying his thick boot to his ribs a few times, he brought him to life again. He then demanded the pistol, upon which the officer, who before had denied any knowledge of it, went directly to a bush but a few feet distant, and pulled it out. They then gave the officer and the other two men a severe drubbing. The owner of the weapons struck one of the men, and unfortunately put his thumb out of joint at the first blow, but it did not prevent him from finishing the castigation, when they left them to make their own reflections.

JULY 27TH. We crossed a high mountain, and came into the valley of the Joaquin, and camped by a small pond. The water was well stocked with fish a foot in length, but we caught but one, as they would only nibble about the hook. Distance 27 miles.

JULY 28TH. The valley opened into a wide prairie before us, apparently boundless, like the ocean. Numerous herds of deer were grazing around us. We saw first a drove of about two hundred wild horses, and afterwards some smaller ones. They curveted their necks, and galloped off as we approached. When we stopped at noon, about half a dozen had the curiosity to come nearer, and look at the mules. Becoming bewildered among the paths of wild horses, we went six miles out of our way, and came to a lagoon that wound through the prairie like a creek, but without a current. Following along its banks for several miles, we camped at night by its side, having lost the main track. There are numerous flocks of ducks and curlews in its waters. Distance, 27 miles.

JULY 29TH. The musquitoes were so annoying in the night, that we got no sleep until we removed our blankets farther from the water. Before starting, some Mexicans passed, going the near way through the valley to the Pueblo-de-los-Angelos, from whom we learned, that we were considerably off track. We then went back and spent the forenoon, along the biou [bayou] in search of a place to cross to the river, being misdirected by some Mexicans, who were camped at a water hole. At four, we returned to that place, and found a trail leading down the river, which was several miles to our right, as indicated by a row of trees. We overtook an American with a herd of cattle, from whom we learned that the ferry was eight or ten miles down the river. We camped a mile from the ferry at 9 o'clock in the evening. I have no where seen game as plenty as in this valley. We killed an antelope in the morning. We could frequently see herds of deer and elk in different directions around us, as well as wild horses. In the lagoons were plenty of geese, ducks, curlews, snipe, and other fowl. We have taken but little pains to kill game, as we do not wish to carry much on our animals, and are not willing to spend any time, but I should suppose that a hunter would find it easy to kill from half a dozen to a dozen antelope or elk in a day, besides a great many birds. The valley of the Joaquin and Sacramento are said to be sixty miles wide. This valley may truly be called a Paradise for hunters.

JULY 30TH. We came to the ferry before breakfast. The river here is not over one hundred yards wide, and all that was asked for each person was two dollars. Some of the animals swim across, but those that chose could have the privilege of leading an animal behind a boat for one dollar and a half. Cole and Evans led each two animals across, for which they bargained for one dollar per animal. The rest after several trials were driven across. Rice went into the water to guide them, and after getting into the current, found it difficult to proceed, or to get back. Temple rushed in, reached him a stick, and thus saved him. The ferryman informed us, that more than a hundred persons generally crossed a day. There are no buildings here, the ferrymen live in a tent. The river banks are beautified with large shade trees, thinly scattered, forming delightful groves. After stopping until 12 o'clock, we entered again upon a prairie, twenty miles across. We reached the Tuolumne river at dark, and encamped.

JULY 31ST. We arrived at the ferry early. It is kept by an American. The river was low, but they asked two dollars for crossing each person. We forded the stream without difficulty, and entered upon another prairie. The Tuolumne is a branch of the Joaquin. We became bewildered among the small paths, and camped at night on the prairie near an arroyo, where we found some water, and used horse chips for fuel.

AUGUST 1ST. Our course from the ferry across the Tuolumne has been north of east; we followed a blind track, and at 10 A.M., after passing through a succession of hills, we came into a large traveled road, at right angles. After consulting awhile as to which was the probable way to Stanislaus, we finally determined to take the right, as we observed that most of the tracks were in that direction. We supposed that we were within two or three miles of Stanislaus, from the distance we had gone, however we traveled several miles in a burning sun, in uncertainty whether we were right, and getting out of water, suffered much from thirst. Finding a little water oozing from the side of a hill, we hastened to taste it, and found it unfit for drinking, containing sulphur. At four in the afternoon we came to a little water in a hole, containing some insects, commonly called *wiggletails;* here we had another *confab,* and Temple, Rice and Evans thinking we were going in the right direction for Stanislaus kept on, and Field, Cole and myself stopped, and camped to wait until some one should pass. In about half an hour a Mexican appeared, from whom we learned that we were wrong. In an hour or two the party that went on returned, having found from some Mexicans, their mistake. We camped at this place.

AUGUST 2ND. Learning that we were now ten leagues from Stanislaus, and about four from the Tuolumne diggings, we determined first to visit Tuolumne. It was one league to the ford and ferry on the river. Before crossing we spent an hour or two with some Americans who had just arrived, and were much discouraged at the prospect. Temple and Rice determined to go back to Stanislaus. The diggings were scattered along up the river, principally three leagues above. The place where we stopped was reached by a very rough mule path, along the steep and rocky bank of the river. There were but few people here, perhaps fifty or more.

I have been more than six months on the journey. As one object in taking this trip was for the travel it afforded, now it is over, I do not regret it, as I think that I have been amply repaid, although I have been exposed to the scorching sun month after month, to hardships and dangers, have lain upon the ground under the open canopy of heaven, and been deprived of the refreshing shade by day, yet my health was never better for the same length of time in my life. All the time while camping out, I have not had a single cold. Goldsmith says,—

> "Man wants but little here below,
> Nor wants that little long."

That he *really* wants but little, especially in a climate like this, where but little clothing is necessary, and where he can sleep on the ground, with a single blanket, as sweetly as in the most sumptuous bed-chamber, and when necessity compels, can partake of a single dish of almost anything eatable that can be had, and quench his thirst with cold water, with a greater relish than the epicure discusses the most costly dainties, and the choisest viands, we all can bear witness who have been over this route.

The greater part of Mexico, through which we have passed, I think undesirable. There are large dry wastes, with now and then a green spot, where there is water. It is distant from the sea-board, and has but few navigable streams. The whole distance from Camargo, nearly three thousand miles. We found it necessary to go in a compact body as a military company. The whole distance most of us carried our guns at our saddle bows, before us; and at night laid them under our blankets by our sides.

AUGUST 5TH. I am happy to find that labor is generally suspended here to-day, (Sabbath). Indeed it seems more like a day of rest, than any for months past. If it were not for some one hammering across the river, it would indeed seem like the Sabbath.

We are among the mountains, whose steep sides in many places come down to the river, so that it is difficult to pass along their sides. There are some small scattered oaks and pines upon the mountain sides. The river is very rapid, with frequent falls, and its bottom rocky.

Wherever there is sufficient room between the mountains, so that the river has changed its channel, or overflows in high water, they are called bars, and here the gold is principally found.

AUGUST 9TH. We have moved two miles further up the river. There are perhaps thirty men on the bar, who are getting an ounce or upwards per day. Occasionally a man is so fortunate as to get several ounces. About a week since, two men got eleven ounces, and one man nine ounces. Some Mexicans obtained twenty ounces in an aroyo, one day this week, just below here.

They are beginning to find gold in the ravines, that lead down the mountain. There is a store near by. Flour is selling at 50 cents, Saleratus $4.00, Beans 50 cents, Sugar 50 cents, Tea $4.00, Dried Meat 50 cents per pounds. Tin pans for washing $16.00, &c. Some have tents, but others prefer sleeping in the open air, as there is no dew, it is as agreeable as any other way.

DECEMBER 3D. I slept in the open air until the last of November, when we had the first rain. I then raised my tent, which I had previously used for a bed. Provisions were lower in the fall, but when the rain set in, rose to $1.00 per pound. The health of the miners has been remarkably good. I have heard of but one death, and that of an intemperate man. The men generally appear to enjoy this kind of a wild life, although home is often spoken of. There certainly can be none more independent. The labor, I have not thus far found harder than farm work. And when our work is over, we cook our meals, and spend our time quietly together. We have had venison all the fall. We have shot deer, standing at our camp. Some western hunters went out about twice a week, and generally killed a grizzly bear. Young cubs were heard playing, nearly every evening, in the thick brushwood at the foot of the mountain. This growth is called jimersal, (I do not know its orthography); it spreads out with thick branches about two feet from the ground, and is almost impenetrable to man, and forms a safe retreat for these animals. A grizzly was killed while passing over the bar.

Our government in the mines is this: Whenever there are new diggings, and a sufficient number of men to require regulations, they hold a meeting and choose an Alcalde, before whom all cases are brought, and who gives decisions as judge. His decisions in all cases that have come under my notice, have been considered valid. The miners pass laws concerning the number of feet of ground each man is entitled to; concerning rights to claims, how long a claim may be left unworked, and held in possession, &c., and the Alcalde sees them executed.

I spent the winter of '49 and '50 in San Francisco. Rented a room in Clay street, 12 by 24 feet, for which I paid $450 per month. The summer of '50 I had business on the Yuba River, and traveled on its three branches from their mouths to the upper cañons.

The sources of these streams are in the Sierra Nevada, (snowy mountains), and the scenery is as nearly Alpine, as any section in America.

There is gold from the mouth of this river, which empties into the Feather, to the sources of its branches.

In the Spring a company of four of us explored the source of the South and Middle Forks of the Yuba River. Having occasion to cross the mountain between the two rivers, we found the snow in many places ten feet deep, and camped at night under some large trees, where there was the least, and then were obliged to dig four feet to the ground to build our fire.

The cañons on the river are from one to eight miles long. They are formed by the river wearing a passage through the rock, which rises in places from fifty to one hundred feet perpendicular. Some of them can be passed by clinging to the ledges, while it is necessary to climb the mountain to pass others. During the summer I traveled considerably on business, alone among the mountains, to pass from one [group of] diggings to another. On one occasion in crossing a mountain to get to the South Yuba, I lost my way, and arrived at the river, at the middle of a cañon, four miles long. Endeavoring to pass down this cañon, night came on, when it became dangerous to move in any direction. After searching for some time for a place to lie down, I at length found one at the lower side of a ledge, where by scraping away the earth, and piling stones at the lower side to prevent my rolling down the precipice into the river, I made my bed for the night.

After spending a considerable portion of 1850 in Mercantile business in Sacramento and Marysville, I arrived at home in March, 1851.

THE END.

Notes

PREFACE

1. William H. Goetzmann and William N. Goetzmann, *The West of the Imagination*, p. 127.
2. John D. Unruh, Jr., *The Plains Across: The Overland Emigrants and the Trans-Mississippi West, 1840–60*, p. 401.
3. Ibid., p. 408.
4. Edwin Bryant, *What I Saw in California, Being the Journal of a Tour by the Emigrant Route and South Pass of the Rocky Mountains, across the Continent of North America, the Great Desert Basin, and through California, in the Years 1846–1847*, p. xiv.
5. Lorenzo D. Aldrich, *A Journal of the Overland Route to California and the Gold Mines*, p. 87.
6. Ibid., map dates.
7. C. W. Haskins, *The Argonauts of California: Being the Reminiscences of Scenes and Incidents that Occurred in California in Early Mining Days by a Pioneer*, pp. 437–38.
8. Ibid., p. 438.
9. Durivage acknowledged traveling with Governor McNees' company prior to his arrival in Janos (Ralph P. Bieber, ed., *Southern Trails to California in 1849*, p. 200).
10. Ibid., p. 171.
11. Glenn S. Dumke, editor of the 1945 edition of George B. Evans's *Mexican Gold Trail*, explained that a "jornada originally meant a one-day's march, but it was taken by western travelers to mean an exceptionally dry stretch of desert country" (p. 165).

BIOGRAPHICAL INTRODUCTION

1. Asa B. Clarke, "A Sketch of the Life of A. B. Clarke before 1849 When He Left for California," pp. 6–7.
2. Ibid., pp. 7–9.
3. Ibid., p. 9.

4. Ibid., p. 10.
5. Ibid., pp. 11, 12, 14.
6. Ibid., p. 15.
7. A. B. Clarke, *Travels in Mexico and California,* p. 134.
8. "Early History around the Grand Parlor City," p. 22.
9. Fanny E. Clarke, "A Short Sketch of Our Branch of the Clarke Family," p. 3.
10. Asa B. Clarke, "Sketch," p. 16.
11. Fanny E. Clarke, "A Short Sketch," p. 4.

FROM NEW YORK TO BRAZOS SANTIAGO

1. S. S. Brooks, according to C. W. Haskins, *The Argonauts,* p. 438.
2. Dr. F. K. Robinson, according to ibid.

TO MONTEREY

1. In August, 1848, Cave Johnson Couts, traveling with Maj. Lawrence P. Graham's wagon train, wrote, "Have never yet been on a march when we came to a town or Ranch that they did not raise a *fandango* if possible, and all dance the livelong night, save those who were so unfortunate as to have to remain in camp" (Henry F. Dobyns, ed., *Hepah, California! The Journal of Cave Johnson Couts from Monterey, Nuevo Leon, Mexico to Los Angeles, California during the Years 1848–1849,* p. 16).
2. John E. Durivage of the New Orleans *Daily Picayune* reported on March 10, just fifteen days later, that one hundred deaths had occurred in Brownsville's population of fifteen hundred. See Bieber, *Southern Trails,* p. 160. The best description of the agonies caused by cholera may be found in the diary of George W. B. Evans, who died in Sacramento City of the disease on December 16, 1850, after suffering off and on since October 26. (His original diary is located in the Huntington Library, San Marino, California.) Many healthy men seemed to die overnight from cholera. Others, such as Audubon, suffered several bouts with it, and survived.
3. Durivage observed a grand religious ceremony in Mier, which was an effort to seek favor from God and consequent exemption from

cholera (Ferol Egan, *The El Dorado Trail: The Story of the Gold Rush Routes across Mexico*, p. 69).

4. Durivage wrote about those smuggling goods into Mexico at Roma and noted that 250 had died of cholera in Camargo by March 24 (Bieber, *Southern Trails*, p. 165).

5. Durivage made extensive recommendations on emigrant needs: "unless a man has four or five hundred dollars in his pocket he had better remain at home" (ibid., pp. 189, 200).

6. Durivage wrote, "This post is under the command of a general who has almost as many officers under him as men. The privates are the dirtiest, seediest, and most ill-conditioned knaves I ever beheld, infinitely worse in appearance than Falstaff's followers ever could have been" (ibid., p. 171).

TO CHIHUAHUA

1. General Ampudia was defeated by American generals Taylor and Worth in the Battle of Monterrey, September, 1846. A stone fort, El Soldado, was built on a hill just to the west of Monterrey *before* the battle there. Clarke may have recorded the location of the fort incorrectly. Otis A. Singletary, *The Mexican War*, pp. 28–46.

2. The derogatory term "greaser" originated during the Mexican War (1846–48).

TO JANOS

1. This marauding had been occurring for many years, and by 1849 the governments of Sonora, Chihuahua, Durango, and Coahuila "were offering payments for Apache and Comanche scalps, the capture of Indian children who could be bartered for kidnapped Mexican children, the rustling of Indian livestock, and the destruction of Indian villages." The payments were in the range of $200 per scalp. A gruesome account of the scalping of a dignified old Indian woman by professional scalp hunter John Glanton is recorded in *El Dorado Trail*, pp. 92–93. George B. Evans, in Chihuahua late in June, 1849, wrote, "Men, Americans, have been induced by offered rewards to go out in companies and kill Indians who are known to be at peace with the Government of the United States, and drive off their mules and

horses, women and children, the latter to be placed in the hands of the Mexicans at from one to two hundred and fifty dollars to be condemned to a life of slavery and wretchedness. It is admitted by all that the Indians have dealt with the Mexicans on this frontier without mercy, but, at the same time, does this furnish the shadow of an excuse for men of my own nation? I think it does not, and I blush for the perpetrators of acts like these, and hope that no evil will result to those little bands of Americans now wending their way through Indian territory." In July, Evans commented that Apaches were "not well-armed, poorly mounted, but thievish in their dispositions; and, unlike the Camanche nation, fight in ambush. The Camanches are braver, have better arms, and are generally well mounted and make their attacks on horseback, and are, perhaps, as a nation the best horsemen in the world" (*Mexican Gold Trail,* pp. 115–16).

2. Doniphan's Missouri volunteers, outnumbered by the Mexicans, were said to be inspired to victory by the sudden appearance of "America's bird," a large bald eagle. It swooped and began circling the battlefield, slowly and majestically. Volunteer John T. Hughes wrote, "the American eagle seemed to spread his broad pinions and westward bear the principles of republican government" (John T. Hughes, *Doniphan's Expedition* [Cincinnati, 1848], pp. 302, 37, quoted in Robert W. Johansen, *To the Halls of the Montezumas: The Mexican War in the American Imagination,* p. 55).

3. In Lt. Col. W. H. Emory's "Notes of a Military Reconnoissance," made with the advance guard of the Army of the West under command of Brig. Gen. Stephen W. Kearny, the following comments, dated October 20, 1846, about Apaches met near the Gila River appear: "[The Apaches came in], headed by their chief, Red Sleeve. They swore eternal friendship to the whites, and everlasting hatred to the Mexicans. The Indians said that one, two, or three white men might now pass in safety through their country; that if they were hungry, they would feed them; or if on foot, mount them. The road was open to the American now and forever. [Kit] Carson, with a twinkle of his keen hazel eye, observed to me, 'I would not trust one of them.' . . . at length the call of 'boots and saddles' sounded. The order, quickness and quietude of our movements seemed to impress them. One of the chiefs, after eyeing the general with great apparent admiration, broke out in a vehement manner: 'You have taken New

Mexico, and will soon take California, Durango and Sonora. We will help you. You fight for land; we care nothing for land; we fight for the laws of Montezuma and for food. The Mexicans are rascals; we hate and will kill them all.' There burst out the smothered fire of three hundred years!" (p. 60).

In October, 1846, Henry Smith Turner, also traveling with Kearny's Army of the West, wrote: "Red Sleeve (frequently called 'Mangas Colorado' or 'Mangas Coloradas,' the Apache Chief has come into our camp (at Rio Mimbres)—he promises good faith and friendship to all Americans, and has kindly offered to furnish guides to Captain Cooke to conduct him by a good route to and down the Rio Gila. The General has made him and his men presents" (Dwight L. Clarke, ed., *The Original Journals of Henry Smith Turner with Stephen Watts Kearny to New Mexico and California, 1846–1847*, p. 85).

In Emory's notes, the following description was given of Apaches: "a large number of Indians had collected about us, all differently dressed, and some in the most fantastical style. The Mexican dress and saddles predominated, showing where they had chiefly made up their wardrobe. One had a jacket made of a Henry Clay flag, which aroused unpleasant sensations, for the acquisition, no doubt, cost one of our countrymen his life. [The Henry Clay flag was a campaign banner used during Clay's presidential race on the Whig ticket in 1844. It had a circle of twelve small stars with one large star in the middle. The name Henry Clay was in large print and the word Frelinghuysen in small print. I gratefully acknowledge the Henry Clay Estate in Lexington, Kentucky, for this information.] Several wore beautiful helmets, decked with black feathers, which, with the short shirt, waist belt, bare legs and buskins gave them the look of pictures of antique Grecian warriors. Most were furnished with the Mexican cartridge box, which consists of a strap round the waist, with cylinders inserted for the cartridges.

"These men have no fixed homes. Their houses are of twigs, made easily, and deserted with indifference. They hover around the beautiful hills that overhang the Del Norte between the 31st and 32d parallels of latitude, and look down upon the States of Chihuahua and Sonora; and woe to the luckless company that ventures out unguarded by a strong force. Their hills are covered with luxuriant grama, which enables them to keep their horses in fine order, so that they can always pursue with rapidity and retreat with safety. The light and graceful manner in which they mounted and dismounted, always upon the right side, was the admiration of all. The children are on horseback from infancy. There was amongst them a poor deformed woman, with legs and arms no longer than an infant's. I could not learn her history, but she had a melancholy cast of countenance. She was well mounted, and the gallant manner in which some of the plumed Apaches waited on her, for she was perfectly helpless when dismounted, made it hard for me to believe the tales of blood and vice told of these people. She asked for water, and one or two were at her side; one handed it to her in a tin wash basin, which from its size, was the favorite drinking cup" ("Notes," p. 61).

Before arriving at Galeana on July 26, Evans observed what he called Aztec ruins. His company was worried about Apaches at the time and he wrote, "Gomaz, the Appache chief, has offered a reward of a thousand dollars for each American scalp, so we may be watching and praying" (*Mexican Gold Trail,* p. 134).

4. At Barranca, Durivage wrote about the wagon master with whom he was traveling (and whom Clarke would join after recuperating in Janos) and the need to watch for Apaches: "Governor McNees, who is one of the 'push' family from Howard county, Missouri, says he shall get up steam on his wagons tomorrow morning by sunrise, when we shall have to keep a bright lookout for Indians as a couple of days will bring us right into the heart of their country" (Bieber, *Southern Trails,* p. 200).

RECUPERATION IN JANOS

1. According to Evans, "This place once contained about eight hundred inhabitants, and these plains were once covered with cattle, horses, and mules, and the mountainsides with sheep and goats; but all of these comforts have been appropriated by the Indians and many of the inhabitants killed or forced to seek safer asylums" (*Mexican Gold Trail,* p. 138).

2. In September, 1848, with Graham's wagon train, Couts described the relationship of the Apaches and the Mexicans at Janos: "The Indians, Apaches, molest the inhabitants very much. . . . At

Janas two days before our arrival, one hundred and fifty Mexicans met thirty Apaches on the suburbs of their town, and another desperate engagement ensued. For hours the battle raged, spears glittered and the swift arrows rattled like a hail storm! "Twas only a place for the Romans of Jana—for hours the tide of battle swung upon a hair. Finally, by exhaustion both parties, by mutual consent, fell back, a treaty was immediately entered into by the Alcalde of Janas, on the part of the inhabitants thereof, and the Apache Chief for six months. . . . Their fear, notwithstanding the six month's treaty, increases daily and daily their little towns are becoming depopulated—families moving farther south and occasionally murders by Indians" (Dobyns, *Hepah, California!* p. 43).

3. According to Egan, "Clarke traveled in good company, as McNees had been a Sante Fé trader and had been in California when gold was discovered. Now he was on his way back with a company that numbered over seventy men, five wagons with four pairs of mules per wagon, and a cavayard of extra mules to replace any that got injured or became too worn out to continue" (*El Dorado Trail,* p. 143).

THROUGH GUADALUPE PASS TO SANTE CRUZ ON GRAHAM'S ROUTE

1. Durivage described Graham's trail as "visible everywhere, and chips, broken wagons, and harness showed that they had suffered some" (Bieber, *Southern Trails,* p. 203). The time of year apparently made a big difference in the smoothness of the journey. On August 5, ten miles from Guadalupe Pass, Evans noted, "Here the trails separated. It is evident that Major Graham's moved directly across the plains and the emigrant trails follow the high ground on its edge. We made the attempt to follow Graham's trail but found it too spongy and deep; consequently, we turned and took the emigrant trail and shortly after found several prairie springs of good water, and the road could not be better than this around this great natural basin" (*Mexican Gold Trail,* p. 142).

2. Cooke, traveling with the Mormon Battalion, missed the Guadalupe Pass and blamed his guides, especially Leroux. He later wrote in his journal, "I have no doubt now but that I saw the upper part of the valley of the proper road the day before yesterday. De-

scribed it to Mr. Leroux and requested him to go and examine it next day, and he replied he had. The direction for it is this: To leave the plain we came from about a mile to the south from our road, and a mile and a half from the old trail; in returning, to keep the dry branch where our road turns to the left to go over high hills; it passes just there, between two high rocks, with a pass less than twenty feet between; and just at this spot is a very large oak with a cross cut in its bark. This is called the pass of Guadalupe. I have no evidence that the same difficulty of a break of the great table land and mountainous descent will not be found to extend to the Gila, and I believe that this is the only wagon pass to the Pacific for a thousand miles to the south. It is the road from Janos to Fronteras, although this is forty miles north of Fronteras" (Ralph P. Bieber, ed., *Exploring Southwestern Trails, 1846–1854*, pp. 126–27).

3. Marguerite Eyer Wilbur wrote in 1936, in a preface to Edwin Bryant's book, "One cause that undoubtedly contributed materially to the immediate popularity of Bryant's volume was the discovery, in January, 1848, of gold in California. *What I Saw in California* immediately placed Bryant in the vanguard of authorities on things in California. The volume was read by thousands, and many a prospective miner carried a copy west in the gold rush. . . . Aware that California, from a literary standpoint, was virtually 'Tierra Incognita,' Bryant kept at that time what is the first complete record of life on the overland trail, and California during the feverish days of the Mexican War that preceded its annexation to the United States of America."

Bryant must have been aware that some men would be suspicious of the authenticity of his reports. In the preface of his book was the following statement: "In the succeeding pages, the author has endeavored to furnish a faithful sketch of the country through which he travelled—its capabilities, scenery, and population. He has carefully avoided such embellishment as would tend to impress the reader with a false or incorrect idea of what he saw and describes. He has invented nothing to make his narrative more dramatic and amusing than the truth may render it. His design has been to furnish a volume, entertaining and instructive to the general reader, and reliable and useful to the travelled and emigrant to the Pacific." Among other passages in this large volume, a graphic description of the fate of the Donner party and General Kearny's task of collecting and interring the remains is recorded (pp. 237–40). Undoubtedly, Clarke gleaned information on many of the missions through which his party would pass, including San Juan and San Luis Obispo (Bryant, *What I Saw in California*, pp. xiii, xiv, xi).

4. When Cooke traveled through this high country, an Apache chieftain named Manuelita came into camp with one his guides, Leroux. "Manuelita had been persuaded only with great difficulty to visit the encampment. Cooke assured the chief of the Americans' friendship, at the same time urging that Apaches and Americans ally themselves in the war against the Mexicans, their common enemy. At Cooke's request, Manuelita promised to bring mules to the battalion's camp for trading.

When the battalion had reached the ruins of the San Bernardino Ranch, "Manuelita and some companions soon appeared. Cooke gave the Indians gifts and spoke again of the Americans' friendship for the Apaches. He explained that as long as the Indians remained friendly, American traders would supply their wants and the United States government would give them annual presents. The Apaches replied with protestations of undying friendship. . . . Trading was not very productive. Cooke got at least one mule; the Apaches wanted only blankets" (Harlan Hague, *The Road to California: The Search for a Southern Overland Route, 1540–1848*, pp. 261, 262).

5. Cooke's battalion experienced difficulties with the wild cattle, also. "The fierce cattle often charged the hunters and were hard to kill. At San Bernardino, a bull that repeatedly charged two hunters was hit six times, any one of which should have been fatal, before it expired. . . . Finally, on December 10, the soldiers fought a regular battle with the wild cattle in the vicinity of the deserted ranch of San Pedro, a satellite of San Bernardino. Some hunters inadvertently had driven a group of bulls toward the column. Some of the animals were shot, and this appeared to enrage the others. Cooke saw what was coming and ordered the volunteers to load their muskets to protect themselves. Then the bulls charged." During the battle two soldiers were seriously injured and two mules gored to death (ibid., pp. 264–65).

6. In George B. Evans, *The Mexican Gold Trail*, (p. 147) Glenn S. Dumke notes, "Santa Cruz was one of the nine frontier posts estab-

lished by the Mexican government to guard northern Sonora, and originally had a population of 1,500. By the time Evans and Bartlett arrived, however, the population had dwindled to about 300. The climate of Santa Cruz was notoriously sickly, and Apache incursions were greatly dreaded, the savages having lost all fear of the town's garrison." See John Russell Bartlett, *Personal Narrative of Explorations and Incidents in Texas, New Mexico, California, Sonora, and Chihuahua connected with the United States and Mexican Boundary Commission, During the Years 1850, 51, 52, and 53*, pp. I: 407–409. In October, 1848, Couts wrote, "St. Cruz is an old and compact ranche, inhabited I may say, by one company of Mexican state troops, though none of them would be taken for soldiers, officers included. The company is 70 or 80 strong, and was once cavalry, mounted lancers, but some three weeks since a party of Apaches made an attack and carried off all their animals but one single mule, and all their clothing. . . . [The citizens] care but little for money, comparatively, and will give what they have for a very small quantity of sugar or soap" (Dobyns, *Hepah, California!* p. 54).

TO THE PRESIDIO OF TEUSON AND ACROSS A DESERT
TO THE GILA RIVER

1. From his own admission that they were following Graham's route, from evidence that the "castle and church" described by Clarke were Tumacacori Mission (flanked by the western slopes of the Santa Rita Mountains), and from the fact that Clarke identifies Durivage's difficulties in surviving desert travel after reaching Tucson, it is obvious that Clarke incorrectly identified the river valley. He traveled north along the Rio Santa Cruz Valley. Cooke had traveled the Rio San Pedro Valley, and, according to Couts, Graham was determined to follow his own route and went north along the Rio Santa Cruz (Dobyns, *Hepah, California!*, p. 55). The village Clarke identified as San Pedro may have been Tubac, and it is likely that the one he identified as San Gabriel was San Xavier del Bac, located nine miles from Tucson.

2. Henry Smith Turner, traveling with Kearny's Army of the West, wrote the following about the country that they (and, later, Clarke) had traversed up to a point somewhere on the Gila River in October, 1846: "It is supposed by some that the United States will

place a high value on this country, as affording a highway from the United States via New Mexico to California: but it is my opinion that a roadway is the last purpose to which this country will ever be applied. It is with difficulty a mule can make its way through it—as for wagons, if they ever reach California it must be by a route entirely different from the one we traveled over. . . . The country is healthy to a degree far surpassing in this respect all parts of the United States and perhaps all other parts of the world—there never was a purer atmosphere than I am breathing at this moment, but having said that there is nothing more to be said in favor of the country. Invalids might live here when they might die in any other part of the world, but really the country is so unattractive and forbidding, that one would scarcely be willing to secure a long life at the cost of living it" (Dwight L. Clarke, *Original Journals,* pp. 89–90).

3. Durivage wrote an excellent account of his "first *jornada*" and near disaster:

"The first *Jornada.* I consider the crossing of this *jornada* of eighty miles an era in my life and shall never forget it to the day of my death. It came very near proving the cause of my stepping out from this sublunary sphere, and that I ever did arrive at the Gila in safety was almost a miracle. Until one has crossed a barren desert without food or water under a burning tropical sun at the rate of three miles an hour, he can form no conception of what misery is. My pen is utterly incapable of properly describing it. Each person, upon starting, had a canteen of two quarts of water, which we thought would be sufficient to last us through. Our course lay nearly due north over as sterile a desert tract of country as it was ever my lot to traverse. By seven o'clock in the morning the heat became excessive and our desire for water commenced. From that hour, the sun increasing in power, every moment became really withering; and we, as well as our animals, panting from exhaustion, stopped at eleven o'clock near some stunted mesquite to rest. The road was mostly level and sandy, but as far as the eye could reach, the vegetation was scanty in the extreme, a few mesquite and the *larrea Mexicana* composing the entire growth. Clouds of dust would arise as we moved along, producing a thirst most difficult to allay. In some places there was a rank growth of a green-stalked weed, destitute of leaves, and so unpalatable that animals will not eat it even when starving. Our beasts were picketed near a patch of very miserable grass, but they preferred to doze in what little shade they could find, so oppressive was the heat.

"At four o'clock we are again in the saddle, having come twenty miles already, determining to push on as rapidly as possible. We traveled until two o'clock at night at the rate of four miles an hour by the light of a beautiful moon, and with the exception of one patch near a dry creek, we saw no grass. On the contrary, for leagues the road ran through a perfectly blasted heath with but here and there a stunted bush. Just such a heath must have been where the weird sisters who so tortured Macbeth used to roam about and perform their horrible incantations. I fully expected to see a circle of 'midnight hags' dancing around a bubbling caldron. Not a sound broke the stillness of the night, except the clatter of our horses' hoofs—not even an owl hooted; and the thieving, skulking wolf never crossed our path. In the sultry and dreadful air that was wafted across the plain in great puffs and gusts, even the hoarse croaking of the raven and the mutter of the vampire would have seemed as sweet as the voice of a nightingale. Our canteens had been drained dry long before midnight, our thirst was intense, and the Gila was still leagues upon leagues distant. Having been told that there was water in a peak of the mountain at a certain pass, I scaled it but found none. At two o'clock we pulled up under a mesquite to take a short snooze and rest the animals. My thirst had increased, and I would cheerfully have given a doubloon for a glass of water. We had made thirty miles from our nooning place.

"The next morning at four o'clock, after two hours' rest, we were again en route. My pony showed evident signs of fatigue and thirst, as did two of the others, and I was very fearful they would cave in before we reached the Gila, which we hoped to do by ten o'clock. They all started off well, however, and we rattled on at the rate of five miles an hour until seven o'clock, when the sun had again begun to exercise its withering influence. My thirst still increased, and my poor beast became so weak that he could not be urged on more than two miles and a half an hour. It was then my real sufferings commenced. Not knowing exactly how far it was to water and seeing nothing but mountains in the distance, it was with difficulty I could keep up. So powerful was the heat of the sun that I found it affecting my head very seriously and rapidly wilting me up. At last what I feared came to pass; the intense heat, the lack of food and water all conspiring, I received a *coup de soleil* [sunstroke]. My brain reeled, my limbs lost all power, my sight grew dim, while the noise of a thousand cataracts rang in my ears. I dropped off my horse and crawled under a mesquite, where I lay speechless for some time. Doctor Brent, alarmed by my state of suffering, from my wild looks, swollen lips covered with froth, and the deathly paleness of my countenance, advised me to keep perfectly quiet. He remained with me for half an hour, when my condition becoming worse and worse, he determined to gallop on and send me back water, which he imagined would relieve me. I thought my time had come and made up my mind to die. I will not pretend to describe what my feelings were at the idea of perishing in that spot. But it was ordained otherwise.

"Sometime after the doctor had started, the Mexican lad who was with me entreated me to go on, as he was dying for water. Weak, enfeebled, and wretched as I was, his condition moved me, and nerving myself for the effort, I mounted my horse again, determined to go on till I dropped in my tracks. Here a kind of Providence came to my aid, for just as my horse refused to go any farther, I discovered a loose mule in the bushes, which proved to be my own property. He had evidently broken away from the wagons. I . . . saddled him and rode on a mile farther, where I was again compelled to stop. Here Mr. Clapp passed me; like myself, he was perishing for water, but was able to push on. After half an hour's rest I made another attempt, although it was with difficulty that I could retain my seat in the saddle. The lamentations of the Mexican boy were most pitiable, and I could not but feel for him, wretched as I was myself. I was endeavoring to persuade him that someone would soon bring us water, but in vain, when a turn in the road revealed a most welcome sight to my eyes. A mile ahead was my black servant, Isaac, on horseback, rushing towards us at a headlong gallop. . . . he looked like an angel. I could hardly believe that I really saw him before I had a canteen of water glued to my lips. Heavens, how delicious was that draught! The nectar of the gods was small beer to it! The relief was instantaneous. I had imbibed the waters of life and once more lived again. With a face beaming with pleasure at having relieved 'de boss,' he assured me that it was but four miles to the Gila and that there was plenty of water.

The Mexican lad emptied the canteen I had given him instanter and was begging like a hound for some of mine. I shared it with him, but still his thirst was unsatiated.

"After a wearisome ride I saw the wagons and the tall cottonwoods of the Gila, and when within half a mile of it, my tired mule smelt the running water. She pricked up her ears, gave one long bray, and struck a bee line for the Gila directly through the thick chaparral. I hung on to her back like death to a deceased African, and away we went like the wind to the banks of the Gila, into which she plunged her head and never raised it till her sides were distended like a hogshead. I dismounted as soon as I was able and settled to the water nearly as greedily as she did—gallons were my portion, certainly! Dr. Brent had reached the river about ten o'clock, but it was two o'clock when I arrived. The scene when the mules and horses first reached the stream was described to me as curious. There was no checking their impetuosity; some of their riders were left hanging in the branches of the trees, some were thrown, and some were pitched headlong into the water. Many suffered quite as much as I did on the route, and some more. Those who came with the wagons suffered least. A sufficiency of water should be packed and the trip made almost entirely by night to prevent all such suffering. Several animals broke down on the road" (Bieber, *Southern Trails,* pp. 213–18).

ALONG GEN. KEARNY'S AND MAJ. GRAHAM'S ROUTES
NEAR THE GILA RIVER TO THE JUNCTION OF THE GILA
WITH THE COLORADO RIVER

1. Emory, with General Kearny in 1846, wrote, "The general gave a letter to Governor (Juan Antonio) Llunas, stating he was a good man, and directing all United States troops that might pass in his rear, to respect his excellency, his people, and their property. Several broken down mules were left with him to recruit, for the benefit of Cook's battalion as it passed along" ("Notes," p. 84).

On December 23, 1846, Cooke wrote, "At the house of the Maricopa chief, Antonio, I stopped and spoke to him. Said I was glad to see him; I had heard he was a great friend of the Americans; that now I wished him to show it; that I had good information that his people had taken up two good mules lost by the general above and many more below this; that I required him to have them delivered up; then I should know he was a friend and should reward him, and also give the people something for their trouble; that I also wanted corn, fat beeves, and mules; that I should remain until midday tommorrow in my camp near him . . . I learn tonight the name of a Maricopa that has taken up the mules, and I shall thus be able, I think to recover them" (Bieber, *Exploring Southwestern Trails*, p. 173). Hague, in *The Road to California*, wrote, "The Pimas proved equal to the trust that Kearny had placed in them. Though the general had left only ten or eleven worn-out mules with the Pimas to be turned over to Cooke, they had thirteen. Apparently, the additional animals had been abandoned by the Army of the West along the Gila and were later retrieved by the Pimas. The two bales of goods left by Kearny also were delivered to Cooke" (Hague, *The Road*, p. 275). Following after Cooke, with Graham's wagon train in November of 1848, Couts wrote, "They represented to the Major that Gen. Kearney and Col. Cook 'gave them very many presents,' that they were exceedingly anxious to see the white men come and live amongst them, to teach them how to make corn, big horses, and every thing they did . . . they stopped the Major at the head of the column and asked him if he could not let them have a thousand or two spades, so that they might have a great deal of corn for the next white men that came along! . . . The Major (glad to say was sober) informed them that we had been at war with Mexico for nearly three years, and were just returning home to California, that we had won: that we came from Mexico and not from the U. States: that we were nearly all naked ourselves, having worn out our clothing in the war, but that if we had come from the U.S. we would of course have many presents for them, that the white men always sent them presents when they had an opportunity. This satisfied the old Red Chieftain, as much as if we had given them all we had" (Dobyns, *Hepah, California!* pp. 67–68).

2. In 1846, Emory reported, "to us it was a rare sight to be thrown in the midst of a large nation of what is termed wild Indians, surpassing many of the christian nations in agriculture, little behind them in the useful arts, and immeasurably before them in honesty and virtue" ("Notes," p. 84). After Clarke's passage through the villages, in November, 1849, Robert Eccleston claimed of the Pimas and Maricopas, "The Indians must be watched very close, notwithstanding Major

Emory speaks so highly of their honesty. But if they did not know how to steal then, they have since learnt, & are now very promising pupils, taking things from right before you. Many articles have been stolen by them" (George P. Hammon and Edward H. Howes, eds., *Overland to California on the Southwestern Trail, 1849: Diary of Robert Eccleston,* pp. 212–13).

3. Emory, on November 10, 1846, wrote that the interpreter to Juan Antonio Llunas, chief of the Pimas, told him the following about the origin of the ruins: "he said, all he knew, was a tradition amongst them, that in bygone days, a woman of surpassing beauty resided in a green spot in the mountains near the place where we were encamped. All the men admired, and paid court to her. She received the tributes of their devotion, grain, skins, &c., but gave no love or other favor in return. Her virtue, and her determination to remain unmarried were equally firm. There came a drought which threatened the world with famine. In their distress, people applied to her, and she gave corn from her stock, and the supply seemed to be endless. Her goodness was unbounded. One day, as she was lying asleep with her body exposed, a drop of rain fell on her stomach, which produced conception. A son was the issue, who was the founder of a new race which build all these houses." The next day, while riding with the interpreter to visit another part of the ruins, Emory "asked him if he believed the fable he had related to me last night, which assigned an origin to these buildings. 'No,' said he, 'but most of the Pimos do. We know, in truth, nothing of the origin. It is all enveloped in mystery'" ("Notes," pp. 82–83). Henry Smith Turner, traveling with the same Army of the West, reported the tradition as follows: "The Pima Indians can give no satisfactory account of the period at which this house was built, or by whom it was occupied. They have a tradition among them in relation to it somewhat to the following purport: that it was occupied by the first man, who was the son of a woman—a most beautiful woman, who lived on a neighboring peak, & who when lying one day on her back, felt a drop of water to fall on her womb, whereupon she conceived & brought forth this son, who was the first man, & who begot a numerous race of men, who tilled the ground, & provided for all his wants, & did homage to him in this house—that his progeny were an extremely wealthy race, & occupied the valley of the Rio Gila for a long distance—ruins of their irrigating

were very perceptible on our route today, showing that they must have cultivated the ground to a considerable extent" (Dwight L. Clarke, *Original Journals,* pp. 107–108).

George E. Stuart and Gene S. Stuart write that the Hohokam lived along the Gila and Salt Rivers nearly twenty-five hundred years ago. "In the language of their modern Pima descendants *hohokam* means 'those that have vanished.' Another Pimas word, *Skoaquik,* names the principal Hohokam site—'Place of the Snakes,' or simply Snaketown. The site of Snaketown takes up about 300 acres of gently rolling open desert southeast of Phoenix on the Gila River Indian Reservation, home of the Pimas. The story of the town and its people lasted from before Christ until after the 12th century; in its course it saw North America's first successful conquest of the desert by irrigation, as early as 300 B.C." (*Discovering Man's Past in the Americas,* p. 114).

An extensive description and illustrations of the Casas Grandes and other ruins along the route are in Bartlett, *Personal Narrative,* pp. 272–83.

4. Emory, in 1846, claimed that "The Indians here do not know the name Aztec. Montezuma is the outward point in their chronology; and as he is supposed to have lived and reigned for all time preceding his disappearance, so do they speak of every event preceding the Spanish conquest as of the days of Montezuma. The name, at this moment, is as familiar to every Indian, Puebla, Apache, and Navajoe, as that of our Saviour or Washington is to us. In the person of Montezuma, they unite both qualities of divinity and patriot" ("Notes," p. 64).

5. Recruiting the animals meant providing food, water and rest for them. During his company's passage through the Indian villages in November, 1849, Eccleston wrote, "On looking over Major Emory's report this morning, together with the rumors of the natives, I am satisfied we will have but little grass hereafter, besides taking into consideration the number of emmigrants that have gone through" (Hammon and Howes, *Overland to California,* p. 212).

6. Clarke must have been ahead of Durivage at this point. On June 6, Durivage wrote that he had traveled past "little villages of the Pima and Maricopa for fifteen or sixteen miles. . . . During the day we had observed a number of columns of smoke in the distance, and in

the afternoon were informed that a party of two hundred Pima and Maricopa had just returned from an Apache hunt, bringing back six scalps and twenty-five prisoners, females and children. We were invited by Calo Azul to cross the river to the Coco Maricopa village to attend the scalp dance, but could not conveniently do so" (Bieber, *Southern Trails*, p. 220).

7. According to Couts, wagons were not left here, but in the desert between the junction of the Colorado and the Gila, and Carrizo Creek. At one of the ranchos, on December 11, he wrote, "This morning the mules were sent back for the wagons (35 in number) left on the desert 67 miles from this place. What a dreadful trip for the poor animals; probably of the 210 sent back 10 will never return. Remonstrated with the Major for sending all of my company mules back, in as much as I had already abandoned my clothing &c for the purpose of getting through with what was most necessary, and which I was enabled to do by the course adopted." There is no mention that the mules ever made it, but the company moved on by December 23 with ten yoke of oxen that had been brought to them (Dobyns, *Hepah, California!* pp. 89–90).

8. The city of Yuma, Arizona, is close to this spot.

ACROSS THE GREAT DESERT
TO CARRIZO CREEK AND OJO GRANDE

1. Durivage wrote, "Mr. Nees does not intend to cross for ten days and has sent his mules back into the country to recruit" (Bieber, *Southern Trails*, p. 225). Perhaps this explains why the men split into so many little groups and proceeded on their own, ahead of McNees.

2. On November 30, 1849, Lorenzo D. Aldrich told how, when they arrived at the river to cross, they "found about thirty American soldiers stationed, who had a ferry over which they transported emigrants at the following rates: wagons $4, mules $1, and men $4. The river here is one hundred and seventy yards in breadth, with a current of about 3½ miles an hour. It is crossed by means of a rope suspended from either bank,—a mode of travel very disagreeable and somewhat dangerous. . . . The Gila empties into the Colorado about one-half a mile above the ferry, nearly at right angles, and just below the place of disemboguement, is a gorge of rocks and sand, which imparts a

somewhat picturesque appearance to the spot. On the top of this the Topographical Engineer has his department, and just below the Lieutenant and Commisary have their quarters. We crossed the river in safety and encamped about two miles from the opposite land" (Aldrich, *Overland Route,* pp. 59–60). In September, 1849, Evans described the river as "about two hundred yards, with a five-mile current, good sloping banks on this side but very bluff and about twelve feet high on the other. The waters from the melting of the snows above are now receding, but have for weeks past been very high. The rise of water in this river and tributaries north commences about the middle of June, and about the last of July or first of August, the snows being melted, the water recedes and a stream of two miles in width is at this time within banks, and about the distance across above spoken of. . . . 'Tis said that there are three crossings and that we now occupy the middle crossing. Here the water is deep all the way over and animals are frequently lost by exhaustion" (*Mexican Gold Trail,* pp. 160–61).

3. Egan wrote that the Argonauts wouldn't listen to warnings about the Colorado Desert. They knew it was 90 or 100 miles across, but thought it would be relatively simple to find Cooke's Wells. "It was going to be a season in Hell. Men and animals would drop alongside each other for lack of water. Cooke's Wells would be hard to find, and if found, would turn out to be all right for a small number of men and mules. But these wells and others never had enough water for the thousands of dry throats and swollen tongues. And some waterholes would be covered with green scum and mosquitos, or might even be polluted by bloated and half-eaten carcasses of dead mules and oxen. Then, as if to make an insane jest of their own time in the sun, some emigrants left a weird sight for others to see. These men mocked death by standing dry, almost mummified horses, mules, and oxen in a line alongside the trail as ghostly markers on a deadly path" (*El Dorado Trail,* pp. 166–67). On November 16, Aldrich described the climb toward the tablelands: "the weather was fine and cool, but on the top nothing met the eye but one arid waste of sand, into which our rolling wagon sunk four or five inches above the felloes. The sand continued to drift badly all day . . . the constant braying of the mules for water during the night, being our serenade" (*Overland Route,* p. 60).

4. In December, 1848, with Major Graham's wagon train, Couts wrote, "Here five wells were dug or cleaned out, and a sufficient quantity of rather brakish water obtained to water all the animals. Great numbers of mules and horses had been left since leaving the Colorado, where the Indians stole some 15 or 20, they having been tracked for a considerable distance.

"The Major, in his wisdom, his sound judgement and discretion, determined to leave what wagons we well could, and send back for them" (Dobyns, *Hepah, California!* pp. 82–83). Evans reached this second well on September 5. It was "sunk in the edge of a large basin, the water about twenty-eight feet below the surface of the desert. This well is very weak, and it required much time to water our animals. . . . The ground is covered with the remnants of property, and it is a perfect boneyard; everything but provisions and firearms can be picked up. This well is very poorly protected against the sands from its sides, and unless some large train is forced by necessity to reconstruct it, there will be little water obtained here" (*Mexican Gold Trail,* p. 163).

THROUGH WARNER'S AND WILLIAMS' RANCHES
TO PUEBLO-DE-LOS-ANGELOS

1. Cooke, who had met with Warner, described him thus: "Warner, the Connecticut man turned California proprietor, is quite a study. He exhibits traits of either character, which may be considered the opposites, of our northern continent." Warner wanted Cooke to take his cattle with him for protection, and Cooke consented to do so if they were rounded up, which they were (Bieber, *Exploring Southwestern Trails,* p. 230). According to Couts, Warner was "a white man, famed for his ability in telling lies, but not surpassed even in this by his notoriety as a rascal. He, Warner, stole my stallion as the horses passed. Luckily for him that it was not known to us until we had left him" (Dobyns, *Hepah, California!* p. 91). Joseph J. Hill, in *The History of Warner's Ranch and Its Environs,* a privately printed book located in the Southwest Museum Library in Los Angeles, wrote about a conversation that Major Shepherd (with whom Benjamin Hayes traveled) had with Warner: "He says, he had from three to four hundred hogs, when Gen. Kearny passed—a fact which, he thinks,

Maj. Emory ought to have mentioned, since he has seen none of them [since then]" (p. 123).

2. Cooke wrote in his journal about this spring and valley: "This is a beautiful little valley, shut in by mountains or high hills on every side. The former are nearly covered with green shrubs, amongst which the rocks show themselves, and are crowned with pine and cedar; the latter with oak and other evergreens, and excellent grass. The grass is just up and the country looks verdant. Some large cottonwoods are leafless, but the mistletoe has lent them a green drapery. The name Agua Caliente comes from a bold spring which issues from fissures in the rock at a temperature of about 170° Fahrenheit. It runs clear and freely, and now sends up clouds of steam for a half mile below" (Bieber, *Exploring Southwestern Trails*, pp. 229–30).

3. The Gold Rush was an economic boom for the rancheros, who supplied beef to the hungry miners. Within three or four years, however, disillusioned miners began leaving the gold fields in search of more certain and more familiar forms of economic endeavor." They squatted on the ranchos, leading to their further destruction (Federico A. Sánchez, "Rancho Life in Alta California," p. 24).

4. Aldrich "met with a Mr. Williams, the owner of a ranche a short distance from this spot, who is from the Gold Mines and related marvelous stories of them. He is from San Diego and gave us all requisite information respecting the route, price of shipping &c." (*Overland Route*, p. 64). On September 16, Evans wrote, "Mr. Williams, the owner of this rancho, is well spoken of and has the reputation of being very benevolent and kind to his countrymen. His farm covers twelve square miles of choice land, and upon this he has at large 12,000 head of cattle and 600 mules and horses, all in fine condition. He tells the emigrants that they are welcome to the beef and that they have only to go out and kill it. If a poor man comes along who has been unfortunate and has lost his mule, Mr. Williams gives him one, and the poor fellow is enabled to go on his way rejoicing and thanking God that he has such a countryman in a strange land."

On September 17, after dining with Colonel Williams, Evans wrote, "I found Colonel Williams to be a native of Pennsylvania and from the town of Wilksbarrey [Wilkes-Barre], open-hearted and free as his native air, and ever ready to render assistance to his countryman. He told us that many of the emigrants had reached here with nothing in the world but the clothes they had on, and that many had suffered hunger for many days, and the only way for him to do was to relieve their most pressing wants and send them on to the mines. He has slaughtered a beef every day for months past and frequently had no beef for his own breakfast the next morning." Evans also reported that "the Colonel has a fine vineyard, and this is surrounded with thrifty [sic] bearing peach trees. At this hacienda he has in operation a large soap factory, all of which sells at about 50¢ per pound. Besides these comforts, he has cultivated by his Indians melons, onions, corn, and Irish potatoes, the last of which he now sells at $4 per bushel" (*Mexican Gold Trail,* pp. 175–77). A record book was kept by Colonel Williams, which served as a register, a record of experiences of the overland travel, and as a clearing house of information for parties that followed. However, it was not begun until July 26, 1849, and thus did not note the Clarke and Field party. *The Record Book of the Rancho Santa Ana del Chino,* transcribed and edited by Lindley Bynum, was the Annual Publication of the Historical Society of Southern California and published in Los Angeles in 1934. A copy is located in the Southwest Museum in Los Angeles.

5. Evans recorded the following mileage from Chihuahua:

From Chihuahua to Yanos it is	212 miles
" Yanos to Santa Cruz	203 "
" Santa Cruz to Tucson	97 "
" Tucson to Piemo Village	95 "
" Piemo Village to crossing of the Colorado River	180 "
" the crossing to El Yseta or first grass	102 "
" El Yseta to Pueblo Los Angeles	177 "
	1,066 miles

(*Mexican Gold Trail,* p. 178).

Bibliography

No PURPOSE would be served by listing all of the many titles I consulted while editing this journal. The titles listed below would be helpful to anyone seeking more information about the 1849 southern trail taken by Clarke or about A. B. Clarke himself.

Aldrich, Lorenzo, D. *A Journal of the Overland Route to California and the Gold Mines.* Edited by Glen Dawson. Los Angeles: Dawson's Book Shop, 1950.

Audubon, John Woodhouse. *Audubon's Western Journal, 1849–1850.* Tucson: University of Arizona Press, 1984.

Bartlett, John Russell. *Personal Narrative of Explorations and Incidents in Texas, New Mexico, California, Sonora, and Chihuahua connected with the United States and Mexican Boundary Commission, During the Years 1850, 51, 52, and 53,* 2 vols. New York: D. Appleton & Company, 1854.

Bieber, Ralph P., ed. *Southern Trails to California in 1849.* Glendale, Cal.: Arthur H. Clark Company, 1937. (This volume contains the letters and journal of John E. Durivage of the New Orleans *Daily Picayune.*)

Bieber, Ralph P., ed., in collaboration with Averam B. Bender. *Exploring Southwestern Trails, 1846–1854.* Glendale, Cal.: Arthur H. Clark Company, 1938. (This volume contains the journal of Lt. Col. Philip St. George Cooke while he was with the Mormon Battalion.)

Bryant, Edwin. *What I Saw in California: Being the Journal of a Tour by the Emigrant Route and South Pass of the Rocky Mountains, across the Continent of North America, the Great Desert Basin, and through California, in the Years 1846–1847.* Santa Ana, Cal.: Fine Arts Press, 1936; reprint, Lincoln: University of Nebraska Press, 1967.

Caughey, John Walton. *Rushing for Gold.* Pacific Coast Branch of the American Historical Association, Special Publication No. 1. Berkeley & Los Angeles: University of California Press, 1949.

Clarke, Asa B. "A Sketch of the Life of A. B. Clarke before 1849
    When He Left for California." Undated, unpublished manuscript.
    (Clarke's daughter, Fanny E. Clarke, added supplementary notes.)
————. *Travels in Mexico and California*. Boston: Wright & Hasty,
    Printers, 1852.
Clarke, Dwight L., ed. *The Original Journals of Henry Smith Turner
    with Stephen Watts Kearny to New Mexico and California, 1846–
    1847*. Norman: University of Oklahoma Press, 1966.
Clarke, Fanny E. "A Short Sketch of Our Branch of the Clarke Fam-
    ily." Independence, Ia., 1936. Unpublished manuscript.
Dobyns, Henry F., ed. *Hepah, California! The Journal of Cave Johnson
    Couts from Monterey, Nuevo Leon, Mexico to Los Angeles, California
    during the Years 1848–1849*. Tucson: Arizona Pioneers' Historical
    Society, 1961.
"Early History around the Grand Parlor City." *The Grizzly Bear* 4,
    no. 6 (April, 1909): 18–22.
Egan, Ferol. *The El Dorado Trail: The Story of the Gold Rush Routes across
    Mexico*. New York: McGraw-Hill, 1970.
Emory, Lt. Col. W. H. "Notes of a Military Reconnoissance, from
    Fort Leavenworth, in Missouri, to San Diego, in California, includ-
    ing Part of the Arkansas, Del Norte, and Gila Rivers," *30th Con-
    gress, 1st Session, Senate Executive Document No. 7*. Washington,
    D.C.: Wendell and Van Benthuysen, Printers, 1848.
Etter, Patricia, ed. *An American Odyssey: The Autobiography of Robert
    Brownlee*. Fayetteville: University of Arkansas Press, 1986.
Evans, George B. *Mexican Gold Trail: The Journal of a Forty-Niner*.
    Edited by Glenn S. Dumke. San Marino, Cal.: Huntington Li-
    brary, 1945.
Goetzmann, William H., and William N. Goetzmann. *The West of
    the Imagination*. New York: W. W. Norton, 1986.
Hague, Harlan. *The Road to California: The Search for a Southern Over-
    land Route, 1540–1848*. Glendale, Cal.: Arthur H. Clarke Com-
    pany, 1978.
Hammon, George P., and Edward H. Howes, eds. *Overland to Cali-
    fornia on the Southwestern Trail, 1849: Diary of Robert Eccleston*.
    Berkeley and Los Angeles: University of California Press, 1950.
Harris, Benjamin Butler. *The Gila Trail: The Texas Argonauts and the
    California Gold Rush*. Edited and annotated by Richard H. Dillon.

Norman: University of Oklahoma Press, 1960.

Haskins, C. W. *The Argonauts of California: Being the Reminiscences of Scenes and Incidents that Occurred in California in Early Mining Days by a Pioneer.* New York: Published for the author by Fords, Howard & Hulbert, 1890. (The copy I studied was located in the California Historical Society's Schubert Hall Library in San Francisco.)

Johannsen, Robert W. *To the Halls of the Montezumas: The Mexican War in the American Imagination.* New York: Oxford University Press, 1985.

Pitt, Leonard. *The Decline of the Californios: A Social History of the Spanish-speaking Californians, 1846–1890.* Berkeley and Los Angeles: University of California Press, 1960.

Sánchez, Federico A. "Rancho Life in Alta California." *Masterkey* (Summer/Fall, 1986): 15–25.

Singletary, Otis A. *The Mexican War.* Chicago: University of Chicago Press, 1960.

Stuart, George E., and Gene S. Stuart. *Discovering Man's Past in the Americas.* Washington, D.C.: National Geographic Society, 1969.

Unruh, John D., Jr. *The Plains Across: The Overland Emigrants and the Trans-Mississippi West, 1840–60.* Urbana: University of Illinois Press, 1979.

will: made by Clarke, *xxvii*

Williams, Colonel, 94–95; mentioned in other journals, 131–32 n.4

Worth, General: mentioned in other journals, 113 n.1; in Monterey [Monterrey], 20

Yumas, 83, 84, 87. *See also* Indians

zequias [acequias], 67, 73

Travels in Mexico and California was composed into type on a Linotron 202 in eleven point Garamond #3 with two points of spacing between the lines. Garamond was also selected for display. The book was designed by Frank O. Williams, composed by G&S Typesetters, Inc., printed by offset lithography by Thomson-Shore, Inc., and bound by John H. Dekker & Sons. The paper on which the book is printed is designed for an effective life of at least three hundred years.

TEXAS A&M UNIVERSITY PRESS   :   COLLEGE STATION